# SWITZERLAND TOUR GUIDE

"Essential Travel Guide To Unveiling the Essence of Swiss Beauty and Adventure. Explore Majestic Alps, Indulge in Swiss Cuisine, and Embark on Thrilling Outdoor Pursuits."

## TAMARA HORAN

Swiss Tr

D1416631

# Introduction

## 1.1 Welcome to Switzerland

Welcome to Switzerland, a country that effortlessly combines natural splendor with cultural wealth. Nestled in the heart of Europe, Switzerland is famous for its stunning landscapes, pristine lakes, towering mountains, and picturesque towns. Whether you're seeking outdoor adventures, visiting charming cities, or immersing yourself in Swiss traditions, this guide will help you make the most of your visit.

Switzerland is a land of diverse experiences, where every area has something unique to offer. From the bustling city streets of Zurich to the tranquil beauty of Lucerne, and from the snow-capped peaks of the Alps to the vineyard-dotted shores of Lake Geneva, you'll discover a captivating mix of urban sophistication and natural wonders.

As you start on your Swiss adventure, you'll be greeted by a warm and welcoming atmosphere. Swiss hospitality is renowned worldwide, and you'll find the locals friendly, helpful, and eager to share their rich history with you.

In this travel guide, you'll find thorough information on the best attractions, activities, accommodations, dining choices, and practical tips to ensure a memorable and enjoyable journey through Switzerland. Whether you're a nature enthusiast, a history buff, a food lover, or simply seeking peace, Switzerland has something for everyone.

Get ready to be captivated by the awe-inspiring Swiss Alps, explore charming villages steeped in history, indulge in world-class Swiss chocolate and cheese, and take on thrilling outdoor adventures. Let this guide be your companion as you navigate the wonders of Switzerland, and may your trip be filled with unforgettable moments and cherished memories.

## 1.2 About the Guide

Welcome to the comprehensive "Switzerland Travel Guide 2023." This guide has been carefully curated to provide you with all the important information you need to plan and enjoy your trip to Switzerland. Whether you're a first-time visitor or a seasoned tourist to Switzerland, this guide aims to be your go-to resource for a memorable and fulfilling experience.

What sets this book apart is its up-to-date information, ensuring that you have the most recent insights into Switzerland's attractions, transportation options, accommodations, and more. Our team of travel experts has meticulously researched and compiled the latest details to make your trip as smooth and enjoyable as possible.

**Here's what you can expect from this guide**:
Comprehensive Coverage: We've split Switzerland into regions, highlighting the unique features and attractions of each area. From Zurich and Eastern Switzerland to Geneva and Western Switzerland, and from the Bernese Oberland to Ticino, we provide detailed information to help you explore the best of what each area has to offer.

**Practical Information**: Our guide includes important travel information such as visa requirements, currency and money matters, language tips, safety guidelines, and health concerns. We also offer help on planning your itinerary, budgeting, and packing tips to make your trip hassle-free.

**Attractions and Landmarks**: Discover the must-visit attractions and landmarks that define Switzerland's beauty and cultural history. From the iconic Matterhorn to the enchanting Château de Chillon, the stunning Lake Geneva to the majestic Rhine Falls, we provide insights and tips to help you make the most of your trips.

**Outdoor Adventures**: Switzerland is a paradise for outdoor enthusiasts, and we'll guide you through the diverse range of activities offered. Whether you're interested in hiking, skiing, mountain biking, paragliding, or exploring Swiss lakes, we'll provide advice and practical information to ensure you have thrilling and memorable experiences.

**Swiss Culture and Heritage**: Immerse yourself in Swiss customs, cuisine, festivals, and arts. Learn about Swiss chocolate and cheese, explore museums and art galleries, and discover UNESCO World history Sites that showcase Switzerland's rich cultural history.

**Accommodation and Dining**: Find guidance on picking the right accommodations, whether you prefer hotels, guesthouses, vacation rentals, or camping sites. Additionally, we'll direct you to the best dining experiences, from traditional Swiss cuisine to foreign flavors, ensuring your taste buds are delighted throughout your journey.

**Practical Tips and Resources**: We'll provide practical tips on topics such as local customs and etiquette, language phrases, tipping, and public holidays. You'll also find a list of useful resources, including tourist information centers, online travel tools, and emergency contacts.

As you start on your Swiss adventure, let this guide be your trusted companion, offering valuable insights and ideas to enhance your travel experience. We wish you a memorable journey filled with breathtaking landscapes, unforgettable moments, and a deep respect for the beauty of Switzerland.

## 1.3 Quick Facts about Switzerland

Before diving into the details of your Swiss trip, let's start with some quick facts about Switzerland that will help you familiarize yourself with this captivating country:

**Geographical Location**: Switzerland is a landlocked country situated in Central Europe. It is surrounded by Germany to the north, France to the west, Italy to the south, and Austria and Liechtenstein to the east.

**Capital City**: The capital city of Switzerland is Bern, known for its well-preserved medieval old town and charming design.

**Official Languages**: Switzerland has four official languages: German, French, Italian, and Romansh. The distribution of languages changes across different regions of the country.

**Safety and Security**: Switzerland is considered a safe location for travelers. However, it is always advisable to take standard measures, such as securing your belongings and being aware of your surroundings.

**Transportation**: Switzerland boasts an excellent transportation system. Trains are known for their efficiency, connecting major towns and picturesque regions. Buses and boats also provide convenient choices for exploring different areas. The Swiss Travel Pass offers endless travel on public transportation.

**Visa Requirements**: Depending on your country, you may require a visa to enter Switzerland. Check the visa requirements well in advance and ensure that your passport is valid for at least six months beyond your planned stay.

**Climate**: Switzerland experiences a temperate climate, with variations based on the region and altitude. Summers (June to August) are generally mild to warm, while winters (December to February) can be cold and snowy, especially in mountainous areas.

**Outdoor Activities**: Switzerland is a paradise for outdoor lovers. From hiking and skiing to mountain biking and paragliding, the country offers a wide range of activities for adventure seekers and nature fans.

**Cultural Heritage**: Switzerland is known for its diverse cultural heritage, influenced by neighboring countries and its own unique customs. Each area has its distinct customs, festivals, and culinary specialties, giving a rich tapestry of experiences.

These quick facts will provide you with a solid foundation as you start on your Swiss journey. Keep them in mind as you delve deeper into the guide, allowing you to make informed choices and fully appreciate all that Switzerland has to offer.

# Essential Travel Information

## 2.2 Visa Requirements

Visa requirements for Switzerland vary based on your nationality, the reason and duration of your visit, and whether your country has a visa-free agreement with Switzerland. Here are some important details to help you understand the visa requirements:

**Schengen Area**: Switzerland is a member of the Schengen Area, a zone comprising 26 European countries that have removed internal border controls. If you hold a valid Schengen visa, it usually allows you to enter Switzerland for tourism or business purposes. The longest stay allowed is 90 days within a 180-day period.

**Visa-Free Travel**: Citizens of certain countries do not require a visa for stays of up to 90 days within a 180-day time. These countries include the United States, Canada, Australia, New Zealand, Japan, South Korea, and many European Union countries. However, it is crucial to check the official Swiss government website or call the Swiss embassy or consulate in your home country to verify if you are exempt from obtaining a visa.

**Visa Application**: If your country is not qualified for visa-free travel, you will need to apply for a Schengen visa at the Swiss embassy or consulate in your home country. The application process usually includes completing an application form, providing supporting documents (such as a valid passport, proof of accommodation, trip itinerary, travel insurance, and financial means), and paying the visa fee.

**Duration and Purpose of Stay**: It's important to determine the purpose and duration of your stay in Switzerland when applying for a visa. Whether you plan to come for tourism, business, education, or other reasons, make sure to provide the necessary documentation and adhere to the specified duration allowed by the visa.

**Visa Processing Time**: Visa processing times can vary based on the embassy or consulate and the time of year. It is advisable to apply well in advance of your planned trip to give sufficient time for the processing of your visa application.

**Long-Term Stays**: If you plan to stay in Switzerland for more than 90 days or have a specific purpose, such as work or study, you may need to apply for a different type of visa or permit. These visas often require extra documentation and have special eligibility criteria.

Remember that visa requirements are subject to change, so it is important to check the official Swiss government website or consult with the Swiss embassy or consulate in your home country for the most up-to-date and accurate information regarding visa requirements for your particular situation.

Ensuring you have the necessary visa or permit before going to Switzerland will help you have a smooth and hassle-free entry into the country, allowing you to focus on enjoying the breathtaking landscapes, cultural experiences, and unforgettable moments that await you.

## 2.3 Currency and Money Matters

When it comes to currency and money problems in Switzerland, here's what you need to know to make your financial transactions smooth and convenient:

**Currency**: The official currency of Switzerland is the Swiss Franc (CHF). It is represented by the symbol "CHF." One Swiss Franc is subdivided into 100 centimes.

**Cash and Cards**: Switzerland is a highly cashless country, and credit and debit cards are widely accepted in most establishments, including hotels, restaurants, shops, and tourist attractions. Major cards such as Visa, MasterCard, and American Express are widely used. Contactless payments and mobile payment apps are also common.

**ATMs**: Automated Teller Machines (ATMs) are easily available in Switzerland, and you can withdraw Swiss Francs using your debit or credit card. ATMs can be found in banks, train stations, shopping centers, and tourist places. Be aware that some ATMs may charge a withdrawal fee, so check with your bank regarding any relevant fees or withdrawal limits.

**Currency Exchange**: Currency exchange services can be found at airports, big train stations, banks, and currency exchange offices in tourist areas. While exchanging cash, be mindful of the exchange rates and any related fees or commissions. It is often more easy to withdraw cash from ATMs using your debit or credit card for better rates.

**Tipping**: Tipping is not required in Switzerland, as a service charge is usually included in the bill. However, it is customary to round up the bill or leave a small tip as a gesture of thanks for good service. If you receive exceptional service, you may choose to give a slightly larger tip, but it is totally discretionary.

**Value Added Tax (VAT)**: Switzerland adds a Value Added Tax (VAT) to most goods and services. The usual VAT rate is 7.7%. However, some items, such as food and books, have a lower VAT rate of 2.5%. When shopping, the displayed prices generally include VAT.

**Foreign Exchange Reserves**: If you plan to visit remote areas or engage in activities where access to banking facilities may be limited, it is advisable to take a small amount of cash in Swiss Francs for emergencies and smaller transactions.

**Budgeting**: Switzerland is known for its high cost of living. It's essential to plan your budget appropriately, taking into account accommodation, meals, transportation, and activities. Consider using a currency conversion app or online tool to estimate costs and ensure you have sufficient funds for your trip.

**Safety and Security**: Switzerland is usually a safe country for financial transactions. However, as with any destination, practice caution when using ATMs or making card payments. Keep an eye on your belongings, use secure ATMs in well-lit areas, and protect your card information when making transactions.

By keeping these currency and money things in mind, you'll be well-prepared to handle financial transactions during your stay in Switzerland. Enjoy your trip with peace of mind, knowing that you have easy options for payments and access to cash whenever you need it.

## 2.4 Language and Communication

Switzerland is a multilingual country, and understanding the language landscape will greatly improve your travel experience. Here's what you need to know about language and conversation in Switzerland:

**Official Languages**: Switzerland has four official languages: German, French, Italian, and Romansh. The distribution of languages changes across different regions of the country.

**German**: German is the most widely spoken language in Switzerland, primarily in the northern and central parts of the country. Swiss German dialects are spoken, which may vary from standard German.

**French**: French is spoken in the western part of Switzerland, especially in the cantons of Geneva, Vaud, Neuchâtel, and Fribourg. It is also widely spoken in cities like Lausanne.

Italian: Italian is spoken in the southern part of Switzerland, in the canton of Ticino, as well as in parts of the Graubünden canton. Lugano and Locarno are famous cities where Italian is widely spoken.

**Romansh**: Romansh is a less-spoken language, mainly in the canton of Graubünden. It is mainly spoken in remote mountain areas.

**English Proficiency**: English is widely known and spoken, especially in tourist areas, major cities, and among younger generations. You can usually communicate in English with hotel staff, tourist information centers, and people in the service industry.

**Tongue Considerations**: It is always polite to learn a few basic phrases in the local tongue. Even a simple "hello," "thank you," or "excuse me" in the local language can go a long way in showing respect and making bonds with locals.

**Language Signage**: Signage in Switzerland is usually in the local language of the region. In tourist places and major transportation hubs, you'll often find signs in multiple languages, including English.

**Language Apps and Translation Tools**: If you want to dive deeper into the local languages or need help with translation, you can use language learning apps or translation tools on your smartphone. These can be helpful for understanding menus, signs, or engaging in simple conversations.

**Cultural Sensitivity:** Switzerland values its linguistic variety, and it is important to respect and appreciate the different languages and cultures within the country. If you are uncertain which language to use, English is usually a safe choice for communication.

**Multilingual Assistance**: If you require assistance or have specific language-related queries, tourist information centers, hotels, and transportation services usually have staff who can converse in multiple languages and provide the necessary support.

Embrace the cultural diversity of Switzerland and try to immerse yourself in the local language and culture. Locals admire the effort, even if you can only speak a few words or phrases. Enjoy the unique experience of interacting with people from different linguistic backgrounds and make meaningful connections during your Swiss journey.

## 2.5 Time Zone and Electricity

Understanding the time zone and electricity standards in Switzerland is important for planning your itinerary and ensuring that your electronic devices work properly.

Here's what you need to know:

**Time Zone**: Switzerland follows Central European Time (CET), which is UTC+1 in normal time. However, during daylight saving time, usually from the last Sunday in March to the last Sunday in October, Switzerland changes to Central European Summer Time (CEST), which is UTC+2. Remember to adjust your clocks accordingly when daylight saving time starts or ends.

**Electricity Standards**: The normal voltage in Switzerland is 230V, and the frequency is 50Hz. Switzerland uses Type C and Type J power outlets. Type C outlets have two round pins, while Type J outlets have three round pins in a row. It is recommended to bring a suitable travel adapter to ensure compatibility with your electronic devices.

**Adapters and Converters**: Depending on your home country's electrical standards, you may need a trip adapter or voltage converter to plug in and use your devices in Switzerland. Most current electronic devices, such as smartphones and laptops, are dual voltage (110-240V) and only require a travel adapter to fit the power outlet shape.

**Accessing Power**: Hotels, accommodations, and public places in Switzerland provide power outlets for charging your gadgets. Most hotels offer a mix of Type C and Type J outlets, while some may have universal outlets that handle various plug types. It's always a good idea to take a travel adapter or power strip to charge multiple devices simultaneously.

**Power Interruptions**: Switzerland has a reliable electricity source, and power interruptions are rare. However, it is recommended to have backup power solutions for important devices, such as mobile phones, especially if you plan to explore remote or mountainous regions.

**Portable Chargers**: If you'll be engaging in outdoor activities or long periods of travel, a portable charger or power bank can be useful for recharging your devices on the go.

Remember to check the power needs of your specific electronic devices and ensure that they are compatible with the Swiss electrical standards. Carrying the necessary adapters and converters will allow you to stay connected, keep your devices powered, and capture memories of your Swiss trip without any hassle.

Additionally, always adhere to electrical safety guidelines, use certified adapters, and practice care when handling electricity to ensure a safe and enjoyable trip in Switzerland.

## 2.6 Safety and Emergency Contacts

Ensuring your safety and being prepared for emergencies

is important when traveling. Familiarize yourself with safety rules and keep important emergency contacts at hand during your time in Switzerland. Here's what you need to know:

**General Safety**: Switzerland is considered a safe place for travelers. However, it is always wise to take common-sense precautions to ensure your well-being. Keep an eye on your belongings, especially in crowded tourist areas and on public transportation. Be cautious of your surroundings, especially at night, and follow your instincts.

**Emergency Services**: In case of an emergency, call the universal emergency number 112 or 117 to reach the police, ambulance, or fire services. These emergency services run nationwide and are available 24/7.

**Travel Insurance**: Prior to your trip, it is highly recommended to purchase comprehensive travel insurance that covers medical emergencies, trip cancellations, lost baggage, and other unforeseen events. Ensure that the insurance policy includes coverage for any specific activities you plan to participate in, such as skiing or hiking in the mountains.

**Medical Facilities**: Switzerland boasts a high level of medical care. In case of non-emergency medical issues, you can visit neighborhood clinics or doctors' offices. If you require urgent medical attention, head to the nearest hospital emergency room. Keep in mind that medical services in Switzerland can be expensive, so having travel insurance is important.

**Mountain Safety**: Switzerland's breathtaking landscapes include majestic mountains that draw outdoor lovers. If you plan to participate in mountain activities, such as hiking, skiing, or mountaineering, it is crucial to be prepared and prioritize safety. Check weather conditions, follow marked trails, inform others of your plans, and carry suitable gear, including maps, navigation tools, proper clothing, and sufficient food and water. It is also suggested to consult local authorities or mountain guides for specific safety information.

**Natural Hazards**: Switzerland experiences natural hazards such as avalanches and rockfalls, especially in mountainous areas. Pay attention to warning signs, follow safety instructions, and ask local authorities or mountain guides for up-to-date information on current conditions.

**Consular Services**: If you require assistance from your home country's embassy or consulate in Switzerland, it is wise to have their contact information readily available. They can provide help in case of lost passports, legal issues, or other emergencies involving your home country.

**Local Laws and Customs**: Familiarize yourself with the local laws and customs of Switzerland to ensure a polite and lawful visit. Be aware of regulations regarding alcohol consumption, drug laws, smoking limits, and other relevant local regulations.

**Personal Safety**: Take steps to safeguard your personal belongings, such as passports, wallets, and electronic devices. Use hotel safes for secure storage and avoid displaying valuable things openly.

Remember, it's always better to be prepared and aware of safety measures and emergency contacts. By staying informed and taking necessary precautions, you can have a safe and enjoyable trip through Switzerland, focusing on the beauty of the country and creating lasting memories.

## 2.7 Health and Medical Facilities

Maintaining your health and being informed of medical facilities in Switzerland is crucial for a smooth and worry-free travel experience. Here's what you need to know about health-related matters:

**Medical Services**: Switzerland has a great healthcare system with high standards of medical care. Hospitals, clinics, and medical facilities are well-equipped and staffed with highly trained pros.

**Travel Insurance**: Prior to your trip, it is important to have comprehensive travel insurance that covers any medical expenses, including emergency medical treatment, hospital stays, and medical evacuation if necessary. Ensure that your insurance policy is valid for the length of your stay in Switzerland.

**European Health Insurance Card (EHIC):** If you are a citizen of a European Economic Area (EEA) member country or Switzerland, it is recommended to keep a valid EHIC. This card allows you to receive necessary healthcare services on the same terms as local residents. However, it is still recommended to have travel insurance as the EHIC may not cover all medical costs or repatriation.

**Pharmacies**: Pharmacies, known as "Apotheke" in Switzerland, are widely available and easily accessible. You can find them in cities, towns, and even in some villages. Pharmacies provide over-the-counter medications, prescription drugs, and health-related information. It is recommended to carry a basic first aid kit with common medications and supplies for minor ailments.

**Prescription Medications**: If you require prescription medications, ensure you bring an adequate supply for the length of your stay. Carry medications in their original packaging, along with a copy of the prescription or a letter from your doctor outlining the medication and dosage. It is also helpful to have the generic names of your medications in case of language difficulties.

**Medical Emergencies**: In case of a medical emergency, dial the emergency number 112 or go directly to the nearest hospital emergency room. Hospitals in

Switzerland provide emergency care and have specialized departments for different medical needs.

**Altitude Sickness**: If you plan to visit high-altitude regions or participate in activities like hiking in the Swiss Alps, be aware of the risk of altitude sickness. Gradual acclimatization, staying hydrated, and avoiding strenuous tasks in the first few days can help minimize the effects. Consult with healthcare professionals if you have any worries or pre-existing medical conditions.

**Vaccinations**: Before traveling to Switzerland, it is suggested to ensure that your routine vaccinations are up to date. Additionally, consult with your healthcare provider or a travel medicine specialist to determine if any specific vaccinations are suggested based on your travel plans and personal health history.

**Water Quality**: Tap water in Switzerland is usually safe to drink and of high quality. However, if you prefer bottled water, it is easily available in stores and supermarkets.

**Allergies and Dietary Restrictions**: If you have any known allergies or dietary restrictions, explain your needs to restaurants, hotels, and food establishments. Swiss cuisine offers a variety of choices, and most places can accommodate dietary preferences.

By being mindful about your health and well-being, you can have a worry-free trip in Switzerland. Remember to carry necessary medications, have adequate travel insurance, and seek medical help when needed. Enjoy the beauty of Switzerland while considering your health and safety.

## 2.8 Customs and Etiquette

Switzerland has its own customs and etiquette practices that are worth familiarizing yourself with to ensure respectful and culturally sensitive exchanges. Here are some key things to keep in mind:

**Greetings**: When meeting someone for the first time, a handshake is the most usual form of greeting in Switzerland. Maintain eye contact and address people using their last names unless asked to use their first name. In more informal situations, a simple "hello" or "bonjour" (French) is acceptable.

**Punctuality**: Swiss people value punctuality, so it is important to arrive on time for appointments, meetings, and social events. Being punctual shows respect for others' time.

**Tipping**: Tipping is not required in Switzerland as a service charge is often included in the bill. However, rounding up the bill or leaving a small tip to show appreciation for good service is standard practice. In restaurants, it is customary to leave a tip of around 5-10% if you are happy with the service.

**Dining Etiquette**: When dining in Switzerland, it is

polite to wait for everyone to be set before starting the meal. Keep your hands on the table, but not your knees. It is considered respectful to finish everything on your plate, as it shows love for the food. If you need to leave the table during the meal, it is customary to say "excuse me" or "pardon" to show your intention.

**Dress Code**: Swiss people usually dress neatly and conservatively. When visiting places of prayer, such as churches or cathedrals, it is respectful to dress modestly. In more formal settings, such as fine eating restaurants or theaters, smart casual attire is appropriate.

**Noise Level**: Swiss culture values tranquility, so it is important to keep noise levels low, especially in residential areas, public transport, and other quiet settings. Avoid loud talks or disruptive behavior that may disturb others.

**Smoking Regulations**: Switzerland has strict smoking regulations, and smoking is usually prohibited in public indoor areas, including restaurants, bars, and public transportation. Look for designated smoking places if you need to smoke, and always dispose of cigarette butts responsibly.

**Recycling and Cleanliness**: Switzerland is known for its dedication to environmental sustainability. Respect local recycling rules by separating your waste into the proper bins. Keep public areas clean and tidy by disposing of trash in designated containers.

**Respect for Nature**: Switzerland's natural beauty is

valued by its people. When exploring outdoor areas, such as national parks or hiking trails, follow marked paths, avoid littering, and respect wildlife habitats. Leave nature as you found it, taking care to protect the environment for future generations.

By embracing Swiss customs and etiquette, you will show your appreciation for the local culture and create positive interactions with the Swiss people. Enjoy your journey through Switzerland while respecting the traditions and ideals of this remarkable country.

# Planning Your Trip

## 3.1 Best Time to Visit Switzerland

Determining the best time to visit Switzerland depends on your hobbies and what you wish to experience during your trip. Here's an outline of the different seasons and their highlights to help you plan your visit:

**Spring (March to May)**: Spring in Switzerland brings blooming flowers, lush green scenery, and milder temperatures. It's a great time for outdoor activities like hiking, cycling, and visiting the cities. However, the weather can be unpredictable, with occasional showers and different temperatures, so pack layers and be prepared for changes.

**Summer (June to August)**: Summer is a popular time to visit Switzerland due to its nice weather, longer daylight hours, and a wide range of outdoor activities. You can enjoy hiking in the mountains, swimming in lakes, and visiting charming towns. This is also the peak tourist season, so expect bigger crowds and higher prices. It is recommended to book accommodations and attractions in advance.

**Autumn (September to November)**: Autumn in Switzerland offers beautiful foliage as the leaves change colors, making picturesque landscapes. The temperatures start to cool, but it is still a nice time for outdoor activities. Autumn is also a quieter season with fewer tourists, making it a good time to explore popular sites without the crowds. However, remember that some mountain activities and attractions may have limited availability or shorter operating hours during this time.

**Winter (December to February)**: Switzerland is famous for its winter sports and snowy landscapes. If you enjoy skiing, snowboarding, or other winter activities, this is the ideal time to come. The Swiss Alps change into a winter wonderland with numerous ski resorts offering excellent slopes and facilities. Christmas markets and festive parties add to the charm of the season. Keep in mind that winter is the high season for skiing, so famous resorts can be crowded, and prices may be higher.

It's important to consider your tastes, weather conditions, and activities you wish to engage in when choosing the best time to visit Switzerland. Keep in mind that the weather can vary within different regions and altitudes, so it's a good idea to check the specific conditions of the places you plan to visit.

Additionally, Switzerland's events calendar is filled with culture festivals, music concerts, and sporting events throughout the year. Checking the event schedule can add an extra layer of excitement to your trip.

Ultimately, Switzerland offers something unique in each season, so whether you prefer winter sports, spring blossoms, summer adventures, or fall colors, you'll find opportunities to create unforgettable memories in this captivating country.

## 3.2 Duration of Stay and Itinerary Planning

The length of your stay in Switzerland depends on your travel tastes, available time, and the experiences you wish to have. Here are some things to consider when planning the duration of your trip and creating an itinerary:

**Interests and Activities**: Consider the activities and sites you want to experience in Switzerland. Are you mainly interested in exploring cities, immersing in nature, indulging in outdoor adventures, or a combination of these? This will help you decide the amount of time you need to allocate to different regions and activities.

**Cities and Regions**: Switzerland offers a diverse range of cities and regions, each with its own special charm. Popular locations include Zurich, Geneva, Lucerne, Interlaken, Bern, and Zermatt. Research the highlights and attractions of each place to decide which ones match with your interests. Consider the time needed to explore each city and the travel time between destinations.

**Outdoor Activities**: If you plan to participate in outdoor activities such as hiking, skiing, or exploring the Swiss

Alps, consider the time needed for these activities. Factor in the length of hikes or the number of ski days you want to enjoy. Keep in mind that some activities are weather-dependent, so flexibility in your itinerary is important.

**Transportation**: Switzerland has an efficient transportation system, including trains, buses, boats, and cable cars. Consider the time needed for traveling between locations and the frequency of connections. Swiss Travel Passes or regional passes can provide convenience and cost savings for extended travel within the country.

**Relaxation and Exploration**: It's important to give time for relaxation and spontaneous exploration. Switzerland's scenic beauty welcomes leisurely walks, lakeside picnics, and simply soaking in the tranquil atmosphere. Don't overcrowd your schedule, but leave room for downtime and unplanned discoveries.

**Seasonal Considerations**: Depending on the time of year you visit, certain activities or sites may have limited availability or different working hours. Consider any specific events or festivals you wish to attend and plan properly.

**Budget and Time Constraints**: Your budget and the time you have available will also play a role in determining the length of your stay. Longer trips allow for a more comprehensive exploration of the country, while shorter visits can focus on specific areas or highlights.

As a starting point, a minimum of 7-10 days is recommended to experience the highlights of Switzerland, providing time for city exploration, mountain adventures, and leisurely experiences. However, if you have more time, extending your stay will provide the chance to delve deeper into the Swiss culture and landscape.

When making your itinerary, strike a balance between must-see attractions and allowing for flexibility. Be realistic about travel times and avoid overpacking your plan. Leave room for spontaneity and the chance to immerse yourself in the serenity and beauty of Switzerland.

Remember, the length of your stay and the itinerary you choose should be tailored to your preferences and travel goals. Whether you have a few days or several weeks, Switzerland offers a wealth of experiences that will leave you with lasting memories of this amazing country.

## Suggested 10-Day Itinerary That Will Allow You to Explore the Best of Switzerland:

Day 1: Zurich

Arrive in Zurich, Switzerland's biggest city.

Spend the day exploring the city's highlights, including the historic Old Town (Altstadt), Zurich Lake, Bahnhofstrasse (one of the world's most exclusive shopping streets), and the Kunsthaus art museum.

Enjoy a leisurely stroll along the Limmat River and indulge in Swiss food at a local restaurant.

Day 2: Lucerne

Take a beautiful train ride to Lucerne, known for its picturesque setting on Lake Lucerne and surrounded by the Swiss Alps.

Explore the well-preserved Old Town, visit the famous Chapel Bridge (Kapellbrücke), and admire the stunning views from the Musegg Wall.

Consider taking a boat trip on Lake Lucerne or a cable car ride to the top of Mount Pilatus for sweeping views.

Day 3: Interlaken and Jungfrau Region

Travel to Interlaken, a famous gateway to the Jungfrau Region.

Embark on an unforgettable day trip to Jungfraujoch, known as the "Top of Europe." Experience the scenic train ride to the highest railway station in Europe, and enjoy breathtaking views of snow-capped peaks, glaciers, and alpine landscapes.

Day 4: Bern

Depart for Bern, the capital city of Switzerland and a UNESCO World Heritage site.

Explore the well-preserved medieval Old Town, visit the Bear Park, and discover Bern's iconic sights, including the Zytglogge (Clock Tower) and the Federal Palace. Take a stroll along the River Aare and enjoy Bern's culinary delights.

Day 5: Zermatt and Matterhorn
Travel to Zermatt, a car-free alpine town famous for its views of the iconic Matterhorn.
Explore the beautiful streets of Zermatt, visit the Matterhorn Museum, and enjoy the Alpine atmosphere.
Consider taking a cable car ride to Gornergrat for incredible panoramic views of the nearby peaks.

Day 6: Montreux and Lake Geneva
Journey to Montreux, located on the shores of Lake Geneva.
Visit the famous Chillon Castle, enjoy a leisurely walk along the lake promenade, and take in the scenic beauty of the area.
Consider a visit to the nearby Lavaux Vineyards, a UNESCO World Heritage site known for its terraced vineyards and beautiful views.

Day 7: Geneva
Head to Geneva, Switzerland's cosmopolitan hub and a center of international relations.
Explore the Old Town, visit St. Pierre Cathedral, and walk along the shores of Lake Geneva.
Discover Geneva's famous landmarks, including the Jet

d'Eau and the Palais des Nations (United Nations headquarters).

Day 8: Lausanne and Swiss Riviera
Travel to Lausanne, a lively city on the shores of Lake Geneva.
Explore the picturesque Old Town, visit the Olympic Museum, and enjoy the city's culture offerings.
Take a scenic boat ride along Lake Geneva to discover the charming towns and villages of the Swiss Riviera, such as Vevey and Montreux.

Day 9: Basel
Depart for Basel, a cultural city set on the banks of the Rhine River.
Explore Basel's art museums, including the Fondation Beyeler and Kunstmuseum, and walk through the charming Altstadt.
Visit the impressive Basel Minster and walk along the Rhine promenade.

Day 10: Departure
Take the time to discover any remaining attractions in Basel.
Depart from Switzerland with unforgettable memories of your trip through this beautiful country.

Remember, this itinerary can be customized based on

your preferences and the exact time of year you visit. Be sure to check the opening hours and availability of sites and consider the use of Swiss Travel Passes or regional passes for convenient transportation throughout your trip. Enjoy your adventure in Switzerland!

## 3.3 Budgeting and Expenses

Budgeting for your trip to Switzerland is important to ensure a smooth and enjoyable experience. The cost of travel in Switzerland can vary based on your travel style, preferences, and the time of year. Here are some estimated costs for luxury, midrange, and budget trip planning:

**Luxury Travel**:

Accommodation: Luxury hotels in Switzerland can range from $300 to $1000+ per night, based on the location and level of luxury.

Dining: Fine dining events at high-end restaurants can cost around $150 to $300 per person for a multi-course meal with wine.

Transportation: Private transfers or first-class train tickets will add to your costs. Budget around $100 to $200 for longer train trips.

Activities: Engaging in exclusive activities like helicopter tours, private boat charters, or spa treatments can cost several hundred dollars or more.

Total Daily Estimate: $500 to $1500+ per person.

## Midrange Travel:

Accommodation: Midrange hotels or guesthouses usually range from $100 to $300 per night, depending on the location and season.

Dining: Enjoying local food at restaurants or cafes can cost approximately $30 to $80 per person for a meal.

Transportation: Utilizing public transportation, such as trains and buses, is a cost-effective choice. Expect to spend around $30 to $80 per day on transportation.

Activities: Participating in guided tours, museum visits, or outdoor activities may run from $50 to $150 per person.

Total Daily Estimate: $150 to $400 per person.

## Budget Travel:

Accommodation: Budget-friendly options like hostels, guesthouses, or budget hotels can run from $50 to $150 per night, based on the location and facilities.

Dining: Eating at affordable restaurants, cafes, or buying food from grocery stores can cost around $15 to $30 per person for a meal.

Transportation: Opting for second-class train tickets or utilizing area transportation passes can help keep costs down. Budget around $20 to $50 per day on transportation.

Activities: Exploring free attractions, hiking in nature, or

exploring local markets can be low-cost or free.
Total Daily Estimate: $70 to $200 per person.

Keep in mind that these estimates are meant as general guidelines, and real costs may vary based on personal preferences, exchange rates, and the specific locations you visit. Additionally, expenses for souvenirs, extra events, and alcoholic beverages are not included in these estimates.

To stay within your budget, consider planning ahead, booking accommodations and transportation in advance, and researching affordable dining choices. Taking advantage of free attractions, exploring nature, and using local transportation choices will help keep costs down.

It's important to note that Switzerland is known for its high standard of living, and prices can be higher compared to some other places. However, with careful planning and budgeting, it is still possible to enjoy a memorable trip to Switzerland within your chosen budget range.

## 3.4 Packing Tips and What to Bring

Packing properly for your trip to Switzerland will ensure you have everything you need for a comfortable and enjoyable stay. Here are some packing tips and essential things to consider:

**Clothing**:

Layered Clothing: Switzerland's weather can be unpredictable, so pack clothes that can be layered for different temperatures. Include items like lightweight shirts, sweaters or fleeces, a waterproof jacket, and a warm coat or jacket for cooler seasons.

Comfortable Shoes: Switzerland is known for its beautiful landscapes, so bring comfortable walking shoes or hiking boots for visiting cities and nature trails.

Swimwear: If you plan to come during the summer or wish to enjoy the country's lakes or thermal baths, pack swimwear.

Formal Attire: If you plan to eat at upscale restaurants or attend special events, consider bringing formal attire.

**Essentials**:

Travel Documents: Bring your passport, visa (if needed), and any necessary travel insurance documents.

Money and Cards: Bring some Swiss Francs in cash for immediate expenses, but credit and debit cards are generally accepted. Notify your bank of your trip plans to avoid any issues with card usage.

Adapter/Converter: Switzerland uses Type J power outlets, so bring a proper adapter if your devices have different plug types. Check if your electronics are suitable with Switzerland's 230V electrical system.

trip Guides and Maps: Consider carrying a trip

guidebook or download relevant apps for easy access to information and navigation.

**Outdoor Gear**:

Daypack: A small backpack is useful for day trips, hiking, and carrying supplies.

Sun Protection: Pack sunscreen, sunglasses, a hat, and lip balm to protect yourself from the sun's rays, especially at higher levels.

Insect Repellent: Depending on the season and location, mosquitoes and other insects may be present, especially near bodies of water or in wooded areas.

Outdoor Gear: If you plan to participate in outdoor activities like hiking or skiing, bring appropriate gear such as hiking boots, rain gear, a hat, gloves, and thermal layers.

**Miscellaneous**:

Medications: If you take any prescription medications, ensure you have an ample supply for the length of your trip. It's also a good idea to bring a simple first aid kit.

tools: Don't forget to pack your camera, phone, chargers, and any other tools you may need. Consider a power bank for charging on the go.

Toiletries: Bring travel-sized toiletries, including toothbrush, toothpaste, shampoo, conditioner, and any other personal care items you enjoy.

**Other Considerations**:

Check the season and weather forecast for your travel dates to pack properly.

Pack a reusable water bottle to stay hydrated throughout your trip.

Consider taking a lightweight travel umbrella or a foldable rain poncho.

Pack a photocopy of important papers in case of loss or theft.

Leave some space in your luggage for items you may want to bring back.

Remember to pack efficiently, prioritize essentials, and consider the activities you plan to participate in when deciding what to bring. Pack based on your personal wants and preferences, and always check the baggage allowance and restrictions of your airline.

Switzerland offers diverse experiences, from city exploration to outdoor adventures, so pack properly to make the most of your trip and ensure a comfortable and enjoyable stay.

## 3.5 Travel Insurance

When it comes to travel insurance, it's important to choose a reputable provider that offers comprehensive coverage for your specific needs. While I cannot provide a complete list, here are some well-known travel insurance companies that you can consider:

**Allianz Global Assistance**: Offers a range of travel insurance plans with different coverage choices, including trip cancellation, emergency medical coverage, and baggage protection.

**World Nomads**: Known for offering travel insurance specifically built for adventurous travelers. They offer coverage for different activities, including hiking, skiing, and water sports.

**Travel Guard**: Provides comprehensive travel insurance plans that cover trip cancellation, emergency medical costs, baggage loss, and more. They also give 24/7 travel assistance services.

**AXA Assistance USA**: Offers travel insurance plans with coverage for trip cancellation, emergency medical costs, baggage protection, and travel assistance services.

InsureMyTrip: Allows you to compare and choose from various trip insurance plans offered by different providers. They provide a convenient platform to customize coverage based on your unique needs.

**American Express Travel Insurance**: Provides travel insurance plans with different levels of coverage, including trip cancellation, emergency medical costs, and baggage protection. These plans are offered to both American Express cardholders and non-cardholders.

Before choosing a travel insurance provider, carefully review the coverage options, policy details, and any exclusions or limitations. Consider factors such as the coverage limits, deductible amounts, medical coverage, emergency assistance services, and the general reputation of the company.

It's important to read the policy wording carefully to understand what is covered and what is not. Additionally, consider factors such as the length of your trip, the activities you plan to participate in, and any pre-existing medical conditions that may require additional coverage.

Remember to compare prices, coverage, and customer reviews to make an informed choice that suits your specific travel needs.

## Local Itinerary Services In Switzerland

When planning your trip to Switzerland, you may consider utilizing local itinerary services that can provide personalized recommendations, assistance with bookings, and expert knowledge of the local sites. Here are a few local plan services in Switzerland that you can explore:

**Swiss Travel Concierge (swisstravelconcierge.com):** Offers tailor-made itineraries and personalized travel planning services. They can help with hotel bookings, transportation arrangements, activity recommendations, and more.

**MySwitzerland (myswitzerland.com):** The official tourism website of Switzerland offers a wealth of information on different destinations, attractions, activities, and events throughout the country. You can find suggested itineraries, travel tips, and useful advice to plan your trip.

**Local Travel Agencies**: There are several local travel agencies based in Switzerland that specialize in building customized itineraries and offering local expertise. These agencies can help plan guided tours, transportation, accommodations, and other travel services based on your preferences. Some examples include Kuoni (kuoni.com) and Switzerland Travel Centre (switzerlandtravelcentre.com).

**Local Tour Guides**: Hiring a local tour guide can be a great way to explore specific areas or attractions in Switzerland. They can provide in-depth information, insider tips, and a personalized experience tailored to your interests. Platforms like ToursByLocals (toursbylocals.com) and Viator (viator.com) offer listings of local guides who can build customized itineraries.

Remember to communicate your preferences, interests, and budget to the itinerary service or local experts to receive the most relevant suggestions. It's also advisable to study and read reviews about the services or people you plan to engage with to ensure their credibility and reliability.

By utilizing local itinerary services, you can benefit from local knowledge and expertise to create a well-rounded and personalized itinerary that fits your travel tastes and allows you to make the most of your time in Switzerland.

# Getting to Switzerland

## 4.1 Airports and Airlines

Switzerland is well-connected to important international destinations through its airports, making it easily accessible for travelers from around the world. Here are some key airports in Switzerland and the companies that serve them:

**Zurich Airport (ZRH)**: Located in Zurich, it is the biggest international airport in Switzerland and a major hub for both domestic and foreign flights. Some airlines that run at Zurich Airport include Swiss International Air Lines (the national carrier), Lufthansa, British Airways, Emirates, Air France, and Delta Air Lines.

**Geneva Airport (GVA)**: Situated in Geneva, it is the second-largest airport in Switzerland. It serves as a gateway to the western part of the country, including famous locations like Geneva, Lausanne, and the Swiss Alps. Airlines active at Geneva Airport include Swiss

International Air Lines, easyJet, Air France, KLM, British Airways, and Turkish Airlines.

EuroAirport                    Basel-Mulhouse-Freiburg **(BSL/MLH/EAP)**: Located near the borders of Switzerland, France, and Germany, this unique airport is jointly run by the three countries. It serves the Basel area and the surrounding regions. Airlines that fly at EuroAirport Basel-Mulhouse-Freiburg include easyJet, Air France, Lufthansa, Swiss International Air Lines, and Ryanair.

**Bern Airport (BRN)**: Situated in Bern, the capital city of Switzerland, this airport mainly serves domestic flights and a few foreign connections. SkyWork Airlines and Helvetic Airways are the major airlines operating at Bern Airport.

**Lugano Airport (LUG)**: Located in Lugano, in the Italian-speaking area of Switzerland, this airport serves as a gateway to the southern part of the country. It offers flights to several places in Europe, mainly through regional carriers.

When planning your trip, consider the proximity of these airports to your chosen destinations within Switzerland. Each airport has excellent transportation connections, including trains and buses, to help you reach your final location.

It's worth mentioning that some airlines offer direct flights to Switzerland, while others may require a layover or connecting flight. Additionally, flight availability and routes may vary based on the time of year and the airline's schedule.

To find the best deals on flights, consider comparing prices and choices on flight search engines such as Skyscanner (skyscanner.com), Kayak (kayak.com), or Google Flights (google.com/flights). These platforms allow you to search for flights based on your chosen dates, airports, and airlines, helping you find the most convenient and affordable choices for your journey to Switzerland.

Remember to check the baggage limits, visa requirements, and any travel restrictions or entry requirements specific to your home country and Switzerland before booking your flights.

## 4.2 Train Travel

Train travel is a popular and efficient way to explore Switzerland, offering scenic routes, convenience, and good connectivity across the country. Switzerland's well-developed train network is known for its punctuality, comfort, and stunning views. Here's what you need to know about train travel in Switzerland:

**Swiss Federal Railways (SBB):** The Swiss Federal Railways (SBB) is the national railway company of

Switzerland and runs the majority of train services within the country. SBB offers a comprehensive network that connects important cities, towns, and tourist destinations across Switzerland.

**Train Types:**
**InterCity (IC) and InterCity tilting (ICT):** These are high-speed trains that link major cities and offer comfortable seating, onboard amenities, and a smooth ride.
**InterRegio (IR):** These regional trains link smaller towns and cities within Switzerland, offering frequent stops and shorter distances.
**RegioExpress (RE) and S-Bahn:** These local trains serve shorter lines and connect suburban areas and smaller towns.
Swiss Travel Pass: If you plan to heavily use train travel during your visit to Switzerland, consider the Swiss Travel Pass. It gives unlimited travel on the SBB network, including scenic routes and some mountain transportation, for a specified duration. The pass also gives free admission to many museums and discounts on different attractions.

## Scenic Train Routes:
**Glacier Express:** This famous train journey takes you on an eight-hour panoramic ride through the Swiss Alps, passing through stunning landscapes, mountain peaks,

and valleys.

**Bernina Express**: It is one of the most scenic train routes in the world, crossing the Swiss Alps and giving breathtaking views of glaciers, mountain passes, and picturesque villages.

**GoldenPass Line**: This route connects Lucerne to Lake Geneva, going through beautiful landscapes, including the Swiss Riviera and the famous resort town of Interlaken.

**Gotthard Panorama Express**: Combining a train and boat ride, this route takes you through the picturesque Gotthard Pass, with stunning views of mountains and lakes.

**Timetables and Tickets**: Train timetables can be easily found through the SBB website or mobile app. Tickets can be bought online, at train stations, or via ticket machines. It is advisable to check the schedules and availability in advance, especially for scenic routes or during peak travel times.

**Luggage**: Swiss trains have specific storage areas for luggage near the entrances and above the seats. There are also larger storage spaces available for oversized or bulky things. Ensure that your luggage is labeled and easily traceable.

**Ease and Amenities**: Trains in Switzerland are known for their ease, cleanliness, and onboard amenities. Many trains offer spacious seating, power outlets, free Wi-Fi (SwissPass holders), and dining or snack choices. Some long-distance trains have panoramic windows to enhance your scenic trip.

**Train Stations**: Swiss train stations are well-equipped with services such as ticket counters, information desks, waiting areas, restrooms, and food outlets. Larger stations often have luggage storage rooms and shops.

Train travel in Switzerland is not only practical but also an experience in itself, giving breathtaking views and a stress-free way to explore the country. With a well-connected rail network, convenient schedules, and comfortable trains, you can enjoy the beauty of Switzerland's landscapes while enjoying a smooth and efficient ride.

## 4.3 Driving in Switzerland

Driving in Switzerland can be a convenient way to explore the country, especially if you want to visit remote places or have more flexibility in your itinerary. Here's what you need to know about driving in Switzerland:

**Driver's License**: To drive in Switzerland, you must have a valid driver's license granted by your home country. International driving permits (IDPs) are usually not needed, but it is recommended to carry one alongside your normal license, especially if it is not in English or a major European language.

## Road Rules and Regulations:

Drive on the right-hand side of the road.

Overtake on the left-hand side.

Adhere to speed limits (usually 50 km/h in urban areas, 80 km/h on country roads, and 120 km/h on highways unless otherwise posted).

Seat belts are required for all occupants.

Children under 12 years old and shorter than 150 cm must use suitable child restraints.

Using a mobile phone while driving is banned unless you have a hands-free system.

It is necessary to have headlights on at all times, even during the daytime.

Strict drink-driving rules are enforced, with a maximum blood alcohol limit of 0.5 g/L.

## Traffic and Parking:

In urban places, be aware of tramlines and pedestrian zones.

Pay attention to parking rules and restrictions, which are often strictly enforced. Look for designated parking places or use public parking garages.

Blue parking zones require a parking disc to display the time of arrival, while white zones normally allow free parking.

**Speed Cameras and Tolls**: Switzerland has an extensive network of speed cameras to police speed limits. Additionally, some roads and bridges may have tolls or require a vignette (toll sticker) to be displayed on your windshield. The vignette can be bought at border crossings, post offices, petrol stations, and online.

**Car Rental Companies**: Switzerland has various car rental companies that offer rental services at airports, train stations, and major towns. Here are some well-known car rental companies in Switzerland:

Hertz (hertz.com)

Avis (avis.com)

Europcar (europcar.com)

Sixt (sixt.com)

Budget (budget.com)

Enterprise (enterprise.com)

When renting a car, consider factors such as the size of the vehicle, rental rates, insurance coverage, fuel policy, and any extra fees or restrictions. It is recommended to book your car in advance, especially during peak travel seasons, and carefully read the terms and conditions of the rental agreement.

**Road Conditions**: Swiss roads are usually well-maintained and offer stunning views, especially in rural and mountainous areas. However, mountain roads can be narrow, winding, and challenging, requiring cautious driving, especially during winter when snow and ice can make driving conditions more difficult. Stay informed about weather and road conditions, and use winter tires or snow chains when needed.

**Environmental Zones**: Some Swiss towns have

environmental zones where specific emission standards must be met to enter. Make sure your vehicle meets the minimum standards if you plan to drive in these zones.

**GPS and Guidance**: GPS devices and smartphone guidance apps are useful tools for getting around Switzerland. Ensure you have updated maps and familiarize yourself with the routes and directions before starting your trip.

Remember to check your car rental company's rules on crossing borders, insurance coverage, and any specific requirements or restrictions. It is also recommended to have proper travel insurance that includes coverage for rental car accidents and liabilities.

Driving in Switzerland can offer a unique and beautiful experience, allowing you to explore the country at your own pace. Just make sure to familiarize yourself with the local traffic rules, drive safely, and enjoy the breathtaking landscapes Switzerland has to offer.

## 4.4Public Transportation within

Switzerland has an efficient and well-connected public transportation system that makes it easy to move within the country. Whether you prefer trains, buses, boats, or trams, here's what you need to know about public transportation options in Switzerland:

**Trains**: Swiss Federal Railways (SBB) runs an extensive train network that covers the entire country. Trains are known for their punctuality, safety, and breathtaking views. You can travel between big cities, towns, and even remote mountain areas using the train system. SBB offers different types of trains, including high-speed InterCity trains, regional trains, and panoramic trains for scenic routes.

**Buses**: Switzerland has an extensive bus network that complements the train system, reaching areas that are not reachable by rail. Regional and local bus routes connect smaller towns, villages, and tourist destinations. PostBus is the largest operator of long-distance buses in Switzerland, offering comfortable and reliable services.

**Trams and Urban Transportation**: Major Swiss towns like Zurich, Geneva, Basel, Bern, and Lausanne have efficient tram and bus systems for urban transportation. These systems provide easy access to attractions, shopping areas, and residential neighborhoods within the cities.

**Boats and Ferries**: Switzerland is home to many beautiful lakes, and boat services are offered on several of them. Lakes Geneva, Lucerne, Zurich, and Thun are popular places for boat cruises, offering stunning views of the surrounding landscapes and access to charming lakeside towns.

**Swiss Travel Pass**: If you plan to use public transportation frequently during your visit to

Switzerland, consider the Swiss Travel Pass. It offers unlimited travel on trains, buses, boats, and even some mountain transportation within a specified duration. The pass also includes free admission to many museums and discounts on different attractions.

**Timetables and Tickets**: Timetables for trains, buses, and boats can be easily viewed through the SBB website or mobile app. Tickets can be bought at train stations, bus stations, ticket machines, or online. Some tickets may have to be validated before boarding the transportation, while others are valid for a set time period.

**Regional Travel Passes**: In addition to the Swiss Travel Pass, different regional travel passes are available for specific areas or scenic routes. These passes offer unlimited travel within a specific region or along designated routes and can be a cost-effective option if you plan to focus your stay on a particular area.

**Transport Apps**: Mobile apps like SBB Mobile, PostBus, and Swiss Travel Guide provide real-time information on schedules, routes, and links. These apps can help you plan your journey, check for any disruptions, and navigate the public transportation system effectively.

Switzerland's public transportation system is famous for its reliability, cleanliness, and ease of use. It helps you to explore the country comfortably while enjoying the beautiful landscapes. Whether you're traveling between cities, visiting smaller towns, or starting on scenic journeys, public transportation in Switzerland offers a convenient and environmentally friendly way to get around.

## How and where to get the passes

To get passes for public transportation in Switzerland, including the Swiss Travel Pass and area passes, you have several options:

**Online Booking**: The easiest and most convenient way to buy passes is through the official websites of the respective passes. For example:

**Swiss Travel Pass**: Visit the official Swiss Travel System website (www.swiss-pass.ch) to book the Swiss Travel Pass online.

**Regional Passes**: Many regional passes have their own dedicated websites where you can find information about the pass, prices, and purchase choices.

**Train Stations**: Passes can be bought at major train stations in Switzerland, including ticket counters and self-service ticket machines. The staff at the train station will be able to help you in choosing the right pass and answering any questions you may have.

**Travel Agencies**: Local and international travel agencies may offer the option to buy Swiss travel passes. Check with established travel agencies in your home country or look for agencies with a presence in Switzerland.

**Swiss Travel System Offices**: Swiss Travel System has authorized sales points where you can buy passes. These include offices found at airports, train stations, and tourist information centers in Switzerland.

**Online Travel Agencies**: Online travel agencies such as Rail Europe (www.raileurope.com) and Swiss Travel Centre (www.swisstravelcentre.com) offer the option to buy Swiss travel passes and regional passes. These platforms provide easy access to a wide range of passes and extra travel services.

When buying your passes, consider the duration of your stay, the places you plan to visit, and the type of travel you intend to do (e.g., city-to-city, regional exploration, or scenic routes). Take note of any terms and conditions associated with the passes, including validity periods, age limits, and any additional benefits or discounts.

It's suggested to book your passes in advance, especially during peak travel seasons, to ensure availability and to save time at the ticket counters. Remember to take your pass with you at all times during your travels in Switzerland, as you may be required to show it upon request by ticket inspectors.

If you have any specific questions or need assistance with buying passes, the official websites or the staff at train stations will be happy to help you make the right choice for your travel needs.

## 4.5 Entry Points and Border Crossings

Switzerland is a landlocked country in the heart of Europe, surrounded by several nearby countries. If you plan to enter Switzerland, here are the key entry points and border crossings to consider:

Airports:

**Zurich Airport (ZRH):** Located near Zurich, it is the biggest international airport in Switzerland and serves as a major hub for both domestic and international flights.

Geneva Airport (GVA): Situated near Geneva, it is the second-largest airport in Switzerland and offers a wide range of domestic and foreign connections.

Basel-Mulhouse-Freiburg Airport (BSL/MLH/EAP): Located near Basel, this unique airport is jointly operated by Switzerland, France, and Germany, making it an excellent choice for travelers in the border region.

Train Connections:

From neighboring countries: Switzerland has good train connections with its neighboring countries, including Germany, France, Italy, Austria, and Liechtenstein. Major cities and towns near the borders have direct train services that allow easy entry into Switzerland.

EuroCity (EC) and InterCity (IC) trains: These high-speed trains connect Swiss cities with major European cities, making it convenient to travel to Switzerland from different destinations.

**Road Border Crossings:**

France: There are numerous road border points between Switzerland and France, including crossings at Geneva, Basel, Lausanne, and Montreux.

Germany: The Swiss-German border has several road crossings, such as Basel, Zurich, Schaffhausen, and Konstanz.

Italy: Border crossings between Switzerland and Italy can be found at places such as Chiasso, Como, and Lugano.

Austria: The Swiss-Austrian border has crossings at Feldkirch, St. Margrethen, and Bregenz.

Schengen Area: Switzerland is part of the Schengen Area, which allows for free movement of people within its partner countries. If you are going from another Schengen Area country, there are usually no immigration checks at the border.

**Customs and Immigration**:

Customs laws: Switzerland is known for its strict customs laws. When crossing the border, be aware of the duty-free allowances for goods and any restrictions on things such as tobacco, alcohol, and food products.

Immigration Requirements: EU/EFTA people can enter Switzerland with a valid national identity card or passport. Non-EU/EFTA citizens usually require a valid passport and may need to obtain a visa depending on their nationality. Check the visa standards in advance to ensure compliance.

It's essential to check the latest entry requirements and regulations, especially considering any travel limits, passport validity, and visa requirements that may be in place. Visit the official websites of the Swiss Federal Customs Administration (www.ezv.admin.ch) and the Federal Office for Migration (www.sem.admin.ch) for up-to-date information.

Remember to have all necessary travel documents ready, including your passport, visa (if applicable), and any supporting documents needed for your entry into Switzerland. Additionally, familiarize yourself with the customs laws to ensure a smooth and hassle-free entry into the country.

# Regions of Switzerland

## 5.1 Introduction to Swiss Regions

Switzerland is divided into several regions, each having its own unique attractions and experiences. Here's a brief overview of the key regions:

**Zurich and Eastern Switzerland**: This region includes the vibrant city of Zurich, known for its culture scene and shopping. Eastern Switzerland offers beautiful scenery, charming towns, and historic sites.

Bernese Oberland and Jungfrau Region: Located in central Switzerland, this region is famous for its dramatic mountain beauty, including the iconic Jungfrau peak. The town of Interlaken serves as a gateway to outdoor activities.

**Lucerne and Central Switzerland**: Home to the picturesque city of Lucerne, this area is surrounded by mountains and lakes. It gives a blend of history, natural beauty, and outdoor activities.

**Geneva and Western Switzerland**: Geneva is a cosmopolitan city known for its international groups and stunning Lake Geneva. Western Switzerland also includes charming places like Lausanne and the scenic Montreux.

**Ticino**: The southernmost area of Switzerland, Ticino has a Mediterranean flair with palm-lined lakeshores and charming Italian-speaking towns like Lugano and Locarno.

**Valais**: Valais is famous for its Alpine landscapes and iconic Matterhorn peak. It offers famous ski resorts such as Zermatt, Saas-Fee, and Verbier.

**Graubünden**: Located in the eastern part of Switzerland, Graubünden is known for its diverse scenery, including the glamorous resorts of Davos and St. Moritz.

These areas offer a range of activities, from outdoor adventures like hiking and skiing to cultural experiences, historical sites, and culinary delights. Each region has its own unique character and attractions, ensuring there's something for every traveler to enjoy.

## 5.2 Zurich and Eastern Switzerland

### a. Zurich City Guide

Zurich, the biggest city in Switzerland, is a vibrant and cosmopolitan destination that blends a rich past with a modern and dynamic atmosphere. Here's a full guide to exploring Zurich:

**Old Town (Altstadt):**
Begin your tour in the charming Old Town, a historic

district filled with narrow cobblestone streets, medieval buildings, and picturesque squares.

Visit Fraumünster Church, famous for its stunning stained glass windows made by renowned artist Marc Chagall.

Explore Grossmünster, a famous Romanesque-style cathedral with panoramic views from its towers.

Stroll along the Limmatquai promenade, which runs along the Limmat River, and enjoy the lively scene and beautiful views.

**Bahnhofstrasse and Shopping**:

Discover Bahnhofstrasse, one of the world's most exclusive shopping streets, lined with expensive boutiques, department stores, and Swiss watch shops.

Explore the stylish shops and galleries in the nearby Niederdorf area, known for its unique fashion and design stores.

**Museums and Cultural Institutions**:

Visit the Kunsthaus Zurich, Switzerland's premier art museum, showing a vast collection of modern and contemporary art, including works by Picasso, Monet, and Chagall.

Explore the Swiss National Museum, housed in a magnificent castle-like building, to learn about Switzerland's history, culture, and customs.

Don't miss the Museum Rietberg, featuring a diverse

collection of art from around the world, especially from Asia, Africa, and the Americas.

**Lake Zurich and Parks**:
Take a leisurely walk along Lake Zurich's promenade, enjoying the scenic views and fresh air.
Visit the Chinese Garden, a tranquil oasis inspired by Chinese architecture and landscaping, great for a peaceful retreat.
Explore the expansive Zurich Zoo, home to a wide range of animals, including elephants, penguins, and snow leopards.

**Culinary Delights**:
Experience Zurich's lively culinary scene by indulging in Swiss specialties such as fondue, raclette, and Swiss chocolate.
Visit the vibrant food market, Markthalle, to taste local produce, cheeses, and gourmet treats.
Explore trendy neighborhoods like Kreis 4 and Kreis 5, where you'll find an array of foreign cuisines, cozy cafes, and trendy bars.

**Day Trips from Zurich**:
Take a short train ride to the charming town of Rapperswil, known as the "City of Roses," with its medieval castle and beautiful lakeside setting.
Visit the Rhine Falls, Europe's biggest waterfall, located

near Schaffhausen, for a breathtaking natural spectacle.

Discover the picturesque town of Winterthur, known for its excellent museums, art collections, and well-preserved historic buildings.

Zurich offers a captivating mix of history, culture, shopping, and natural beauty. Whether you're exploring its historic landmarks, indulging in culinary delights, or immersing yourself in its vibrant arts scene, Zurich promises a memorable and enriching experience for every tourist.

## B. St. Gallen

St. Gallen, located in eastern Switzerland, is a charming city with a rich past, a well-preserved old town, and renowned cultural institutions. Here's a full guide to exploring St. Gallen:

### Abbey of St. Gall (Stiftsbibliothek):

Begin your visit at the Abbey of St. Gall, a UNESCO World Heritage Site and one of Europe's most important monastic sites.

Explore the Abbey Library (Stiftsbibliothek), home to a large collection of ancient manuscripts and books, including the famous Codex Sangallensis.

Admire the impressive Baroque building of the Abbey Church, with its stunning interior and intricate stucco work.

**Old Town**:
Wander through the charming streets of St. Gallen's Old Town, filled with beautifully kept medieval and Renaissance buildings.
Visit the Abbey District, where you'll find the Abbey area and other historical buildings like the Abbey Cathedral and the Abbey Courtyard.
Explore the picturesque Rathaus (Town Hall) and the nearby Marktgasse, a lively street lined with shops, cafes, and restaurants.

**Textile Museum and Textile Industry:**
Discover St. Gallen's rich textile heritage at the Textile Museum, which displays the city's history of lace and embroidery production.
Learn about the intricate textile methods, view exquisite lacework, and explore temporary exhibitions on textile arts.
Visit the nearby Vadian Museum, which focuses on the culture history of St. Gallen and the region.

**Gallusplatz and Shopping**:
Explore Gallusplatz, a lively square in the heart of St. Gallen, surrounded by ancient buildings, cafes, and shops.
Enjoy shopping in the city center, where you'll find a

mix of foreign brands, local boutiques, and specialty stores.

Don't miss the weekly farmers' market, held on the Marktplatz, where you can buy fresh local produce and regional products.

**Natural Beauty and Outdoor Activities**:

Take a relaxing stroll in the tranquil Stadtpark, a beautifully landscaped park with gardens, fountains, and statues.

Enjoy a walk or a cable car ride up the nearby Santis Mountain, offering breathtaking panoramic views of the Swiss Alps.

Visit Lake Constance (Bodensee), located a short distance from St. Gallen, and enjoy its scenic shores, boat trips, and water sports activities.

**Events and Festivals**:

Check the city's event calendar for festivals and cultural events, such as the St. Gallen Festspiele (performing arts festival) or the St. Galler Fest (traditional summer fair).

Attend a concert or performance at the St. Gallen Theater, known for its diverse schedule of theater, opera, and musicals.

St. Gallen combines history, culture, and natural beauty, providing tourists with a delightful mix of experiences. Whether you're exploring its historic landmarks, immersing yourself in its textile history, or simply enjoying the city's relaxed ambiance, St. Gallen promises a memorable and enriching visit.

## C. Appenzell

Appenzell is a picturesque town set in the rolling hills of northeastern Switzerland. Known for its traditional Swiss charm, colorful facades, and gorgeous natural landscapes, Appenzell offers a delightful escape. Here's a full guide to exploring Appenzell:

**Appenzell Historic Village:**
Begin your tour in the Appenzell Historic Village, a well-preserved area with charming wooden houses adorned with intricate paintings and ornate balconies.
Take a leisurely walk through the small streets, lined with boutiques, cafes, and souvenir shops.
Visit the Appenzell Museum to learn about the region's history, customs, and native way of life.

**Landsgemeindeplatz:**
Discover the Landsgemeindeplatz, the central square of Appenzell, where the unique open-air democratic meeting known as the Landsgemeinde takes place.
Admire the beautiful Rathaus (Town Hall) with its distinctive frescoes and step inside to see the historic council room.
Appenzell Folklore Museum:
Explore the Appenzell Folklore Museum, which displays

the rich cultural heritage of the area through exhibits on traditional costumes, crafts, and customs.

Learn about the unique Appenzell customs, including folk music, yodeling, and the famous Appenzeller cheese.

**Appenzeller Brewery**:

Visit the Appenzeller Brewery, known for producing the flavorful Appenzeller beer. Take a guided tour to learn about the brewing process and enjoy a tasting of their different beer varieties.

Ebenalp and the Wildkirchli Caves:

Take a cable car ride to Ebenalp, a scenic mountain in the Appenzell Alps offering panoramic views of the nearby landscape.

Explore the Wildkirchli Caves, a network of natural caves that were once used as hermitage and now house a small church and a museum.

**Appenzell Hiking Trails**:

Embark on one of the many hiking trails in the Appenzell area, which offer breathtaking views of the rolling hills, meadows, and forests.

The Alpstein area, with its rugged peaks and serene mountain lakes, offers an array of hiking choices for nature enthusiasts.

Swiss Traditional Food:

Indulge in traditional Appenzell food, such as hearty

Alpine dishes, cheese fondue, and raclette.
Sample the famous Appenzeller cheese, known for its unique flavor, and visit a local cheese dairy to learn about the cheese-making process.

**Local Festivals and Events**:
Check the local event schedule for traditional festivals and events, such as the Appenzell Village Festival, where you can experience traditional music, dancing, and costumes.

Appenzell invites you to immerse yourself in its rich history, stunning landscapes, and warm hospitality. Whether you're exploring the historic village, indulging in traditional cuisine, or going on scenic hikes, Appenzell promises an authentic Swiss experience that will leave you enchanted.

## 5.3 Bernese Oberland and Jungfrau Region

The Bernese Oberland and Jungfrau Region is a stunning mountainous area in central Switzerland known for its majestic peaks, charming alpine towns, and breathtaking natural beauty. Here's a short overview of this captivating region:
**Bern**:
The main city of Switzerland, Bern, serves as the gateway to the Bernese Oberland and Jungfrau Region.

Explore the historic Old Town, a UNESCO World Heritage Site, with its well-preserved medieval buildings and charming arcades.

Visit the famous Zytglogge (Clock Tower) and the impressive Bern Cathedral.

Enjoy the vibrant mood of the Bundesplatz (Federal Square) and take in panoramic views of the city from the Rosengarten (Rose Garden).

**Interlaken**:

Nestled between Lake Thun and Lake Brienz, Interlaken is a famous tourist destination and a hub for outdoor activities.

Experience adrenaline-pumping activities like paragliding, skydiving, and canyoning.

Take a leisurely boat ride on Lake Thun or Lake Brienz and soak in the beautiful mountain scenery.

**Jungfrau Region**:

The Jungfrau Region is famous for its iconic mountain peaks, including the Eiger, Mönch, and Jungfrau.

Explore the picturesque alpine towns of Grindelwald, Wengen, and Lauterbrunnen, which serve as excellent bases for outdoor adventures.

Ride the Jungfrau Railway, known as the "Top of Europe," to reach the Jungfraujoch, the highest railway station in Europe, giving breathtaking views and an Ice Palace to explore.

**Outdoor Activities**:

Hiking: Discover numerous hiking trails that wind

through lush meadows, dense woods, and along mountain ridges, offering stunning views at every turn.

Skiing and Snowboarding: The region offers excellent skiing and snowboarding chances with well-groomed slopes and panoramic vistas.

Water Sports: Enjoy water sports like swimming, kayaking, and paddleboarding on the crystal-clear lakes.

**Schilthorn and Piz Gloria**:

Take a cable car to the top of Schilthorn and visit the revolving restaurant, Piz Gloria, made famous by the James Bond movie "On Her Majesty's Secret Service."

Marvel at the sweeping views of over 200 mountain peaks, including the famous Eiger, Mönch, and Jungfrau.

**Trummelbach Falls**:

Discover the beautiful Trummelbach Falls, a series of impressive waterfalls cascading inside the mountain in Lauterbrunnen Valley.

Take an elevator and walkways to explore the interior of the falls and experience the sheer power of nature.

The Bernese Oberland and Jungfrau Region is a paradise for nature lovers, adventure seekers, and those wanting awe-inspiring mountain vistas. With its charming towns, thrilling outdoor activities, and breathtaking landscapes, this region offers an unforgettable Swiss experience.

# A. Bern

Welcome to Bern, the capital city of Switzerland and a UNESCO World Heritage Site. Bern is known for its well-preserved medieval architecture, charming old town, and rich past. Here's a very detailed guide to touring Bern:

### Zytglogge (Clock Tower):

Start your visit at the iconic Zytglogge, the Clock Tower that goes back to the 13th century.

Witness the complex astronomical clock, which performs an entertaining show every hour.

Climb to the top of the tower for panoramic views of Bern's city.

### Old Town (Altstadt):

Explore the Old Town, a well-preserved medieval neighborhood with narrow cobblestone streets and sandstone houses.

Stroll along the Kramgasse, the main street of the Old Town, lined with shops, bars, and arcades.

Admire the beautiful waterfalls, including the famous Kindlifresserbrunnen (Child Eater Fountain) and the Zähringerbrunnen.

### Bern Cathedral (Münster):

Visit the Bern church, a magnificent Gothic church that dominates the city's skyline.

Climb the tower for panoramic views of Bern and the

nearby Bernese Alps.

Explore the interior of the church and marvel at its stained glass windows and intricate stone carvings.

### Bear Park (Bärenpark):

Discover Bern's symbol, the bear, at the Bear Park located alongside the Aare River.

Observe the bears in their natural environment, explore the outdoor enclosures, and learn about their conservation.

### Bundeshaus (Federal Palace):

Take a guided walk of the Federal Palace, the seat of the Swiss Federal Assembly and the Federal Council.

Learn about Switzerland's political system and enjoy the grand architecture of the building.

### Rosengarten (Rose Garden):

Visit the Rosengarten, a beautiful park with over 200 kinds of roses.

Enjoy panoramic views of Bern's Old Town, the Aare River, and the faraway Bernese Alps.

Relax in the calm surroundings and have a picnic on the hillside.

### Museums and Galleries:

Explore Bern's rich culture scene by visiting its numerous museums and galleries.

The Zentrum Paul Klee shows the works of the famous Swiss artist, while the Bern Historical Museum offers insights into the city's past.

The Museum of Communication, the Alpine Museum, and the Museum of Fine Arts are also worth a visit.

**Shopping and Dining**:

Shop for Swiss souvenirs, luxury goods, and local products in the charming shops and stores of Bern.

Taste classic Swiss cuisine, including cheese fondue, raclette, and rösti, at the city's restaurants and cafes.

Don't forget to try the Bernese specialty, Berner Platte, a hearty dish with different meats and sausages.

**Events and Festivals**:

Check the city's event schedule for festivals and events throughout the year, including the Bern Carnival (Fasnacht) and the Bern Jazz Festival.

Experience the vibrant atmosphere, parades, and cultural acts during these festive occasions.

Bern is a city that seamlessly mixes history, culture, and natural beauty. With its stunning architecture, captivating attractions, and warm hospitality, Bern offers a unique and unforgettable experience for guests.

## B. Interlaken

Welcome to Interlaken, a picturesque town set between two stunning lakes, Lake Thun and Lake Brienz, in the heart of the Swiss Alps. Known as the adventure capital of Switzerland, Interlaken offers a perfect mix of breathtaking natural landscapes, outdoor activities, and Swiss charm. Here's a very detailed guide to visiting Interlaken:

## Höheweg:

Start your visit by taking a walk along Höheweg, Interlaken's main promenade.

Enjoy the beautiful flower fields, shops, cafes, and restaurants lining the street.

Take in the panoramic views of the nearby mountains, including the famous Eiger, Mönch, and Jungfrau.

## Outdoor Activities:

Interlaken is a paradise for outdoor enthusiasts, offering a wide range of adventure sports.

Paragliding: Soar above the mountains and lakes, getting breathtaking views of the Swiss Alps.

Skydiving: Experience an adrenaline rush by skydiving over the picturesque scenery.

Canyoning: Explore the beautiful canyons, rappel down waterfalls, and jump into crystal-clear pools.

White-Water Rafting: Navigate the rapids of the nearby rivers for an exciting water journey.

**Jungfrau Railway**:

Embark on a trip to the "Top of Europe" by taking the Jungfrau Railway.

Travel through picturesque alpine landscapes to reach the Jungfraujoch, the highest train station in Europe.

Enjoy panoramic views from the viewing deck, visit the Ice Palace, and learn about the region's history and glaciers at the exhibition.

**Lake Thun and Lake Brienz**:

Take a leisurely boat ride on Lake Thun or Lake Brienz, surrounded by majestic mountains and charming towns.

Enjoy the serene atmosphere, soak in the stunning scenery, and stop at beautiful lakeside towns like Spiez and Brienz.

**Harder Kulm**:

Ride the funicular or hike up to Harder Kulm, a viewpoint giving panoramic views of Interlaken and the surrounding lakes and mountains.

Visit the restaurant at the top and enjoy a meal while taking in the breathtaking scenery.

**Interlaken's Adventure Parks**:

Test your skills and have fun at one of Interlaken's amusement parks.

Adventure Park Interlaken offers thrilling rope courses, zip lines, and bungee jumps.

Seilpark-Matten offers tree-top adventures and obstacle

courses suited for all ages.

**Swiss Cuisine**:
Indulge in traditional Swiss food at the numerous restaurants and cafes in Interlaken.
Try Swiss favorites like cheese fondue, raclette, and rösti, made with locally sourced ingredients.
Don't forget to taste the tasty Swiss chocolates and enjoy a cup of Swiss coffee.
Shopping:
Explore Interlaken's shopping streets, where you can find Swiss watches, chocolates, gifts, and outdoor gear.
Visit the Höhematte Park, where local artisans often present their crafts and products.

**Festivals and Events**:
Check the local event calendar for festivals and events going during your visit to Interlaken.
The Unspunnenfest, held every 12 years, is a traditional event celebrating Swiss folklore, sports, and culture.
The Greenfield Festival and the Trucker & Country Festival are popular music events held yearly.
Interlaken captivates tourists with its natural beauty, thrilling adventures, and warm hospitality. Whether you're seeking adrenaline-pumping activities, beautiful landscapes, or a relaxing getaway, Interlaken has something for everyone. Immerse yourself in the Swiss Alps and make unforgettable memories in this charming

alpine town.

## C. Jungfrau Region

Welcome to the Jungfrau Region, a breathtaking mountainous region in Switzerland renowned for its majestic peaks, picturesque alpine towns, and pristine natural beauty. Here's a very detailed guide to help you experience the highlights of the Jungfrau Region:

### Grindelwald:

Begin your journey in the charming town of Grindelwald, nestled at the base of the famous Eiger North Face.

Take a cable car or cogwheel train to the top of First, where you can enjoy panoramic views and start on thrilling activities like ziplining and mountain carting.

Explore the village center, dotted with classic Swiss chalets, restaurants, and shops.

Don't miss a visit to the Grindelwald Glacier, where you can watch the stunning ice formations and learn about glacial geology.

### Wengen:

Experience the tranquility of Wengen, a car-free town perched on a sunny plateau.

Enjoy the idyllic atmosphere, take leisurely walks through meadows, and marvel at the surrounding mountain views.

From Wengen, take the Wengernalp Railway to Kleine Scheidegg, a mountain pass giving stunning views of the Eiger, Mönch, and Jungfrau.

**Lauterbrunnen:**
Discover the beautiful valley of Lauterbrunnen, often referred to as the "Valley of 72 Waterfalls."
Marvel at the impressive Staubbach Falls, which falls over 300 meters from a sheer cliff.
Explore the charming village center, lined with traditional Swiss houses and backed by towering cliffs.
From Lauterbrunnen, take the cable car to Grütschalp and then the train to Mürren, a car-free village giving stunning views of the surrounding peaks.

**Jungfraujoch:**
A feature of the Jungfrau Region is the Jungfraujoch, often referred to as the "Top of Europe."
Board the Jungfrau train, an engineering marvel, and ascend to the highest train station in Europe.
At the Jungfraujoch, enjoy panoramic views of snow-capped peaks, visit the Ice Palace with its ice sculptures, and explore the Sphinx Observation Deck for breathtaking sights.
Learn about the history and science of the area at the exhibition inside the mountain.

**Hiking and Outdoor Activities:**

The Jungfrau Region offers a multitude of hiking trails ideal for all levels of experience.

Explore beautiful routes like the Eiger Trail, Schynige Platte Panorama Trail, or the Männlichen to Kleine Scheidegg hike.

Engage in outdoor activities like mountain biking, paragliding, and rock climbing, surrounded by beautiful alpine landscapes.

**Mürren**:

Immerse yourself in the alpine charm of Mürren, a peaceful village set on a terrace above the Lauterbrunnen Valley.

Enjoy panoramic views of the Jungfrau, Mönch, and Eiger peaks, and take leisurely walks through the town and its surrounding meadows.

Visit the Allmendhubel, reachable by funicular, and experience the alpine flower garden and hiking trails.

**Traditional Swiss Culture**:

Experience traditional Swiss culture in the Jungfrau Region by joining folk festivals and events.

Learn about Swiss culture, folklore, and traditional music at events like the Unspunnen Festival, held every 12 years.

Sample classic Swiss cuisine, such as cheese fondue and raclette, in local restaurants and mountain huts.

The Jungfrau Region is a paradise for nature lovers,

adventure enthusiasts, and those wanting a peaceful mountain retreat. Immerse yourself in the awe-inspiring beauty of the Swiss Alps and make lifelong memories in this enchanting region.

## 5.4 Lucerne and Central Switzerland

Lucerne and Central Switzerland offer a harmonious blend of stunning landscapes, rich history, and culture treasures. Here's an outline of what awaits you in this captivating region:

**Lucerne**:
Discover the charming city of Lucerne, set on the shores of Lake Lucerne.
Stroll along the picturesque Chapel Bridge (Kapellbrücke), one of Switzerland's most iconic sites.
Explore the well-preserved Old Town with its cobblestone streets, medieval architecture, and bright buildings.
Visit the renowned Lion Monument (Löwendenkmal), a poignant sculpture that honors the Swiss Guards who lost their lives during the French Revolution.
Enjoy a leisurely boat ride on Lake Lucerne, surrounded by stunning mountain scenery.

**Mount Pilatus**:
Embark on an unforgettable trip to Mount Pilatus, often

referred to as the "Dragon Mountain."

Take a scenic boat ride across Lake Lucerne and then climb to the summit using the world's steepest cogwheel railway.

Enjoy panoramic views from the top, explore the walking trails, and experience the exhilarating Dragon Ride cable car.

**Rigi Mountain**:

Experience the "Queen of the Mountains," Mount Rigi, known for its sweeping views and natural beauty.

Reach the summit by cogwheel train or cable car and enjoy stunning views of Lake Lucerne and the surrounding Alps.

Explore the hiking trails, visit the Rigi Kaltbad mineral baths, or simply relax and take in the quiet atmosphere.

**Lake Lucerne**:

Discover the beauty of Lake Lucerne, surrounded by mountains and dotted with lovely lakeside towns.

Take a scenic boat cruise and enjoy the postcard-perfect views of the lake and its surroundings.

Explore the idyllic towns of Weggis, Vitznau, and Beckenried, known for their tranquility and natural charm.

**Swiss Museum of Transport**:

Delve into the interesting world of transportation at the

Swiss Museum of Transport in Lucerne.

Learn about the history of Swiss innovation in different modes of transportation, including trains, planes, automobiles, and more.

Engage in interactive exhibits and discover the vast collection of vintage cars.

**Central Swiss Alps**:

Central Switzerland is a paradise for outdoor fans and nature lovers.

Embark on amazing hikes in the Swiss Alps, surrounded by majestic peaks and pristine alpine landscapes.

Discover the stunning beauty of Engelberg, Andermatt, and the Uri Alps area, offering a wide range of outdoor activities, including skiing, snowboarding, hiking, and mountain biking.

**Swiss Culture and Traditions**:

Immerse yourself in Swiss customs and folklore in Central Switzerland.

Attend traditional fairs and events, such as the Lucerne Carnival (Fasnacht) or the Alphorn Festival.

Experience real Swiss cuisine, including cheese specialties like raclette and fondue, in local restaurants.

Lucerne and Central Switzerland are a perfect blend of natural wonders, cultural history, and warm hospitality. Whether you're wanting historical landmarks, outdoor adventures, or simply a peaceful retreat, this region has something for everyone.

## A. Lucerne City Guide

Welcome to Lucerne, a picturesque city set in the heart of Switzerland. Known for its stunning lake, charming Old Town, and grand mountain views, Lucerne offers a wealth of experiences and attractions. Here's a very detailed guide to help you discover the highlights of Lucerne:

### Chapel Bridge (Kapellbrücke):

Start your trip by visiting the iconic Chapel Bridge, one of Lucerne's most famous landmarks.

Admire the beautifully preserved covered wooden bridge, which goes back to the 14th century.

Walk across the bridge and enjoy the panoramic views of the Reuss River and the nearby architecture.

### Lion Monument (Löwendenkmal):

Pay a visit to the Lion Monument, a moving sculpture carved into a rock face.

Marvel at the impressive lion sculpture, which honors the Swiss Guards who lost their lives during the French Revolution.

Take a moment to admire the artistry and symbolism of this touching memorial.

### Lake Lucerne (Vierwaldstättersee):

Enjoy the natural beauty of Lake Lucerne, one of Switzerland's most stunning lakes.

Take a leisurely boat cruise and soak in the panoramic views of the surrounding mountains and charming lakeside towns.

Engage in water sports like swimming, paddleboarding, or renting a rowboat to explore the lake at your own pace.

**Musegg Wall (Museggmauer):**

Discover the well-preserved medieval city walls of Lucerne, known as the Musegg Wall.

Walk along the ramparts and enjoy panoramic views of the city and the faraway Alps.

Don't miss the chance to explore some of the nine towers that are open to the public, such as the Zytturm with its famous clock.

**Mount Pilatus**:

Embark on a memorable trip to Mount Pilatus, often called the "Dragon Mountain."

Take a boat ride on Lake Lucerne to Alpnachstad, where you can board the steepest cogwheel train in the world.

Enjoy breathtaking views as you climb to the summit and take in the panoramic vistas of the surrounding Alps.

**Culture and Arts**:

Lucerne is known for its vibrant culture scene, with

numerous festivals, concerts, and events throughout the year.
Visit the KKL Luzern (Lucerne Culture and Convention Centre), an architectural masterpiece featuring world-class performances and exhibitions.
Explore the Richard Wagner Museum, dedicated to the famous composer, and enjoy classical music events at the Lucerne Festival.

Lucerne offers a perfect blend of history, natural beauty, and culture experiences. With its enchanting landscapes and rich history, this city is sure to leave you with unforgettable memories of your Swiss journey. Enjoy exploring the beauty and charm of Lucerne!


## B. Mount Pilatus

Welcome to Mount Pilatus, one of Switzerland's most iconic mountains and a must-visit destination for wildlife lovers and adventure enthusiasts. Rising majestically over Lake Lucerne, Mount Pilatus offers breathtaking panoramic views, exciting activities, and a serene alpine atmosphere. Here's a very thorough guide to help you make the most of your visit to Mount Pilatus:

**Getting to Mount Pilatus**:
Start your trip by taking a boat ride from Lucerne to Alpnachstad, located at the base of Mount Pilatus.

Alternatively, you can take a train to Alpnachstad or Kriens, and then continue with the cogwheel railway or cable car.

**Cogwheel Railway Experience**:
Hop aboard the Pilatus train, the steepest cogwheel train in the world, for an exhilarating and scenic ride.
Marvel at the engineering marvel as the train ascends the steep slopes, giving panoramic views of the surrounding landscapes.
Admire the changing views, including lush green fields, alpine forests, and rugged cliffs.

**Panoramic Cable Car Ride**:
For an alternative adventure, take the Panorama Gondolas or the Dragon Ride cable car from Kriens to Mount Pilatus.
Enjoy the aerial ride as you ascend through the pristine mountainous terrain, with stunning views unfolding below you.

**Summit Experience**:
Once you reach the top, prepare to be captivated by the awe-inspiring views that stretch across the Swiss Alps.
Explore the various viewpoints and terraces, giving 360-degree views of the surrounding peaks, lakes, and valleys.
On a clear day, you may even catch a glimpse of the

faraway Black Forest in Germany and the Vosges Mountains in France.

**Hiking and Nature Trails**:
Embark on one of the many hiking trails that crisscross Mount Pilatus, catering to different fitness levels and tastes.
Wander through alpine meadows, cross forested roads, and soak in the tranquility of nature.
Don't miss the famous Pilatus-Kulm to Fräkmüntegg hike, which takes you through stunning landscapes and offers picturesque views.

**Adventure Activities**:
If you're seeking an adrenaline rush, engage in thrilling activities at Fräkmüntegg, located halfway up Mount Pilatus.
Experience the exhilarating Pilatus Rope Park, a high ropes course giving challenges for all skill levels.
Take a ride on the summer toboggan run, zooming down the track and enjoying the bends and turns.

**Culinary Delights**:
Indulge in the delicious Swiss food at one of the restaurants and mountain huts on Mount Pilatus.
Sample area specialties, including hearty alpine dishes and Swiss desserts.
Pair your meal with a refreshing beverage while savoring

the stunning views from the dining places.

**Overnight Stays**:
For an extraordinary experience, try spending a night on Mount Pilatus at the Pilatus Kulm Hotel.
Enjoy the peace and tranquility of the mountain, watch stunning sunsets and sunrises, and take advantage of the serenity after the day-trippers have left.

**Seasonal Highlights**:
Mount Pilatus offers different views throughout the seasons.
In winter, enjoy skiing and snowboarding on the slopes, while in summer, take advantage of the pleasant weather for outdoor activities.
Keep an eye out for special events and festivals that take place on Mount Pilatus, including concerts and cultural shows.
Mount Pilatus is a true gem of Switzerland, giving an unforgettable alpine adventure. Whether you choose to hike, soak in the views, or participate in thrilling activities, the experience will leave you in awe of the natural beauty that surrounds you. Enjoy your time on Mount Pilatus!

## C. Rigi Mountain
Welcome to Rigi Mountain, often referred to as the "Queen of the Mountains." Located in Central

Switzerland, Rigi is a majestic peak that offers amazing panoramic views, charming alpine landscapes, and a wealth of outdoor activities. Here's a very complete guide to help you make the most of your visit to Rigi Mountain:

**Getting to Rigi Mountain**:
Start your journey by getting a train from Lucerne to either Vitznau or Arth-Goldau, the two main access points to Rigi.
From Vitznau, you can catch the Rigi Bahn, a cogwheel railway that takes you to the summit.
From Arth-Goldau, you can take the Rigi Bahn or choose to hike up one of the well-marked tracks.

**Rigi Bahn Experience**:
Embark on a scenic train ride aboard the Rigi Bahn, one of Switzerland's longest mountain railways.
Marvel at the stunning views as the cogwheel train winds its way up the mountain, passing through woods and meadows.
Enjoy the nostalgic charm of the vintage carriages and the interesting engineering of the cogwheel system.

**Panoramic Views**:
Upon reaching the summit, prepare to be captivated by the breathtaking panoramic views that stretch across the Swiss Alps and nearby lakes.

Take in the beauty of Lake Lucerne, Lake Zug, and Lake Lauerz, along with the snow-capped slopes and rolling hills.

Capture the stunning landscapes from different viewpoints and observation decks.

**Hiking and Nature Trails**:

Rigi Mountain offers an extensive network of hiking trails that cater to all levels of fitness and hobbies.

Choose from easy strolls, moderate hikes, or challenging summit climbs, each giving its own unique perspectives of the surroundings.

Explore the alpine fields, forests, and rocky terrain as you immerse yourself in the natural beauty of the mountain.

**Sunrise and Sunset Experiences**:

For a truly magical experience, try witnessing the sunrise or sunset from Rigi Mountain.

Ascend early in the morning to catch the first rays of sunlight illuminating the scenery, creating a breathtaking spectacle.

In the evening, watch as the sun dips below the horizon, sending a warm glow over the mountains and lakes.

**Winter Activities**:

During the winter months, Rigi Mountain turns into a winter wonderland offering a range of activities.

Enjoy skiing, snowboarding, or tobogganing on the well-groomed hills.
Take a scenic snowshoeing or winter hiking excursion, finding the serene beauty of the snow-covered landscapes.

**Wellness and Spa**:
Relax and rejuvenate at one of the wellness centers on Rigi Mountain.
Pamper yourself with a spa treatment, indulge in a sauna session, or relax in an outdoor hot tub while taking in the magnificent views.

**Culinary Delights**:
Refuel and recover at one of the mountain restaurants or cozy Alpine huts on Rigi Mountain.
Savor traditional Swiss dishes, such as cheese fondue, hearty soups, and alpine favorites.
Don't forget to try the famous Rigi Käse (Rigi cheese), a local specialty made from the milk of cows grazing on the mountain meadows.
Rigi Mountain is a true paradise for nature lovers, offering a wide range of activities, stunning views, and a peaceful alpine ambiance. Immerse yourself in the beauty of this iconic Swiss mountain and make memories that will last a lifetime. Enjoy your time on Rigi Mountain!

# 5.5 Geneva and Western Switzerland

Welcome to Geneva and Western Switzerland, an area known for its stunning natural landscapes, vibrant cities, and rich cultural heritage. Here's an overview of what this area has to offer:

**Geneva**:

Geneva is a cosmopolitan city located on the shores of Lake Geneva. It is famous for its diplomacy, luxury watchmaking, and vibrant cultural scene.

Explore the historic Old Town (Vieille Ville), with its cobblestone streets, charming cafes, and beautiful buildings.

Visit the famous Jet d'Eau, a large water fountain that shoots water 140 meters into the air, and stroll along the scenic lakefront promenade.

Discover Geneva's rich history and tradition by visiting landmarks like St. Pierre Cathedral, Place du Bourg-de-Four, and the United Nations Office.

Don't miss the chance to indulge in Swiss chocolate and sample local culinary delights.

**Lausanne**:

Lausanne is a dynamic city located on the shores of Lake Geneva, known for its picturesque setting and vibrant culture scene.

Visit the Olympic Museum, which showcases the past and spirit of the Olympic Games.

Explore the charming Old Town (Vieille Ville), with its narrow streets, medieval buildings, and lively cafes.

Enjoy a leisurely stroll along the Ouchy promenade, giving panoramic views of the lake and the French Alps.

Lausanne is also home to numerous art galleries, museums, and theaters, making it a hub for art and culture.

**Montreux**:

Montreux is a scenic town set on the shores of Lake Geneva, famous for its annual jazz festival and picturesque surroundings.

Take a leisurely walk along the Montreux promenade, lined with beautiful flowers, statues, and breathtaking views of the lake.

Visit Chillon Castle, a medieval fortress set on a small island near Montreux, and discover its rich history and architectural beauty.

Explore the terraced vineyards of Lavaux, a UNESCO World Heritage Site, and indulge in wine tasting at local farms.

Montreux is also a gateway to the beautiful Swiss Riviera, where you can enjoy boat cruises, water sports, and outdoor activities.

The Geneva and Western Switzerland region offers a perfect mix of natural beauty, cultural experiences, and city charm. Whether you're exploring the vibrant city of Geneva, immersing yourself in the cultural scene of

Lausanne, or enjoying the serenity of Montreux, this region is sure to leave you with unforgettable memories of your Swiss trip.

# A. Geneva City Guide

Welcome to Geneva, a city known for its international diplomacy, beautiful lakefront setting, and cosmopolitan ambiance. Here's a very thorough guide to help you make the most of your visit to Geneva:

### Old Town (Vieille Ville):
Start your tour of Geneva by visiting the charming Old Town, characterized by its narrow cobblestone streets and historic buildings.
Discover St. Pierre Cathedral, an iconic landmark with panoramic views of the city and the nearby Alps.
Explore Place du Bourg-de-Four, the largest square in Geneva, lined with cafes, restaurants, and boutique shops.
Visit Maison Tavel, the oldest house in Geneva, which now serves as a museum showcasing the city's past and development.

### Jet d'Eau and Lake Geneva:
Don't miss the famous Jet d'Eau, a water fountain located in Lake Geneva that shoots water 140 meters into the air. It's one of Geneva's most famous sights.

Take a leisurely stroll along the lakefront promenade, known as the Quai du Mont-Blanc, and enjoy the picturesque views of the lake, the Jet d'Eau, and the nearby mountains.

Consider taking a boat cruise on Lake Geneva to further appreciate the beauty of the area and visit nearby towns and attractions.

**International Organizations**:

Geneva is known as the diplomatic capital of the world, hosting numerous international groups and institutions.

Explore the United Nations Office at Geneva (UNOG), where you can take a guided walk and learn about global diplomacy.

Visit the Red Cross and Red Crescent Museum, which highlights the humanitarian work carried out by these groups.

Discover the Palais des Nations, the European headquarters of the United Nations, and explore its beautifully landscaped grounds.

**Museums and Galleries**:

Geneva boasts a vibrant culture scene with a wide range of museums and galleries to explore.

Visit the Museum of Art and History (Musée d'Art et d'Histoire), housing an extensive collection of artworks, artifacts, and archaeological shows.

Discover the Museum of Natural past (Muséum

d'Histoire Naturelle) and learn about the region's diverse flora, fauna, and geological past.

Explore the Patek Philippe Museum, dedicated to the art of watchmaking, showing a remarkable collection of timepieces throughout history.

**Shopping and Dining**:

Geneva is a paradise for shoppers, having a wide range of luxury boutiques, designer brands, and Swiss watch shops.

Explore the upscale shopping area of Rue du Rhône, known for its exclusive shops and high-end fashion brands.

Indulge in Swiss culinary treats at one of Geneva's many restaurants, cafes, and chocolateries. Don't forget to try the famous Swiss cheese fondue and Swiss sweets.

**Outdoor Activities**:

Take advantage of Geneva's beautiful surroundings and engage in outdoor sports.

Enjoy a leisurely bike ride along the promenades or rent a paddleboat to discover Lake Geneva.

During the summer months, you can relax on the city's public beaches or take a cooling swim in the lake.

Geneva is also a gateway to the nearby Jura Mountains, giving opportunities for hiking, skiing, and snowboarding.

Geneva offers a captivating blend of history, culture, natural beauty, and foreign flair. Immerse yourself in its cosmopolitan atmosphere, discover its rich heritage, and enjoy the stunning vistas of Lake Geneva. Your time in Geneva is sure to be an amazing experience.

# B. Lausanne

Welcome to Lausanne, a vibrant city set on the shores of Lake Geneva. Known for its picturesque setting, rich history, and cultural scene, Lausanne offers a charming mix of old-world charm and modern sophistication. Here's a very detailed guide to help you make the most of your visit to Lausanne:

**Olympic Museum**:
Start your trip by visiting the Olympic Museum, a must-see attraction for sports enthusiasts and history buffs.
Explore the interactive exhibits, showing the history and spirit of the Olympic Games.
Learn about the achievements of Olympic players, view unique memorabilia, and even try out some sports simulations.

**Lausanne Cathedral**:
Visit the majestic Lausanne Cathedral, one of the city's

most iconic sites.

Marvel at the stunning Gothic architecture and detailed details of the cathedral's interior.

Climb to the top of the tower for sweeping views of Lausanne and Lake Geneva.

**Ouchy Promenade**:

Take a leisurely walk along the scenic Ouchy promenade, located on the shores of Lake Geneva.

Enjoy the picturesque views of the lake, the French Alps, and the beautifully landscaped grounds.

Relax at one of the lakeside bars or restaurants, and soak in the tranquil atmosphere.

**Collection de l'Art Brut**:

Art lovers should not miss the Collection de l'Art Brut, a unique museum dedicated to outsider art.

Discover extraordinary artworks made by self-taught artists, often with unconventional techniques and perspectives.

Explore the thought-provoking exhibitions that challenge traditional ideas of art.

**Olympic Park**:

Explore the sprawling Olympic Park, home to several sports venues and the International Olympic Committee headquarters.

Take a tour of the Olympic Museum's grounds, including the Olympic flame, the athletes' village, and different sculptures.

Enjoy the green areas, go for a jog, or simply relax in this tranquil setting.

### Flon District:

Immerse yourself in the lively atmosphere of the Flon district, Lausanne's trendy and artistic neighborhood.

Discover the converted warehouses and factories that now house trendy bars, cafes, shops, and art galleries.

Experience the lively nightlife scene, with a range of bars, clubs, and live music venues.

### Lausanne Old Town (Vieille Ville):

Explore Lausanne's charming Old Town, with its narrow, winding streets and well-preserved medieval buildings.

Admire the historic buildings, including the impressive Palais de Rumine, which houses several museums and cultural institutions.

Discover hidden gems like Place de la Palud, a bustling area with a medieval fountain and a lively market.

### Wine Tasting in Lavaux:

Take a short trip from Lausanne to the nearby Lavaux farms, a UNESCO World Heritage Site.

Enjoy a wine tour and tasting in this picturesque wine-growing region, known for its terraced vineyards facing Lake Geneva.

Sample the local wines, learn about the winemaking

process, and soak in the beauty of the nearby landscapes. Lausanne gives a perfect blend of history, culture, and natural beauty. Immerse yourself in its vibrant atmosphere, explore its rich history, and enjoy the stunning views of Lake Geneva. Your time in Lausanne is sure to be a unique experience.

# C. Montreux

Welcome to Montreux, a charming town set on the shores of Lake Geneva. Known for its picturesque setting, mild climate, and world-renowned jazz festival, Montreux offers a delightful mix of natural beauty, cultural attractions, and a relaxed atmosphere. Here's a very detailed guide to help you make the most of your visit to Montreux:

**Montreux Promenade**:
Start your tour by taking a leisurely walk along the Montreux promenade, known for its stunning views of Lake Geneva.
Admire the meticulously kept flower beds, sculptures, and elegant Belle Époque buildings that line the waterfront.
Enjoy the fresh lake breeze, watch the boats sail by, and take in the panoramic vistas of the lake and the nearby mountains.

### Chillon Castle:

Visit the magnificent Chillon Castle, a medieval fortress set on a small rocky island near Montreux.

Explore the well-preserved castle, with its centuries-old halls, towers, and gardens.

Learn about the castle's rich past, including its connections to the House of Savoy and famous literary figures like Lord Byron.

### Montreux Jazz Festival:

If you visit during the summer, don't miss the world-famous Montreux Jazz Festival, held yearly in July.

Enjoy an incredible lineup of international jazz, blues, and rock performances in different venues throughout the town.

Immerse yourself in the vibrant atmosphere of the event and experience the magic of live music.

### Freddie Mercury Statue:

Pay homage to one of Montreux's most famous residents, the legendary singer Freddie Mercury.

Visit the Freddie Mercury Statue, located along the promenade, which serves as a tribute to the famous lead singer of Queen.

Take a moment to reflect on his contributions to the music business and snap a photo with the statue.

**Lavaux Vineyards**:

Take a short trip from Montreux to the nearby Lavaux vineyards, a UNESCO World Heritage Site.

Explore the terraced vineyards, which run along the hillsides facing Lake Geneva.

Enjoy wine tasting at local wineries, where you can taste the region's renowned wines, including Chasselas, a popular white wine grape variety.

**Montreux Old Town**:

Discover the beauty of Montreux's Old Town, located uphill from the lakefront.

Wander through the narrow streets lined with historic buildings, shops, and cafes.

Visit the Church of St. Vincent, a beautiful medieval church with stunning stained glass windows and a peaceful setting.

**Vevey**:

Just a short distance from Montreux, visit the nearby town of Vevey, known for its picturesque setting and cultural sites.

Explore the historic Old Town, filled with charming squares, bars, and art galleries.

Visit the Alimentarium, an interesting food museum dedicated to the history, culture, and science of food.

**Lake Cruises and Water Activities**:

Take advantage of Montreux's setting on Lake Geneva and enjoy a boat cruise on the lake.
Marvel at the beautiful scenery, including the Swiss and French Alps, while gliding across the clean waters.

Engage in water sports such as paddleboarding, kayaking, or swimming during the summer months.
Montreux is a place of enchantment, where natural beauty meets cultural wealth. Immerse yourself in the serene atmosphere, explore the attractions, and enjoy the lively music scene. Your time in Montreux is sure to be a unique experience.

## 5.6 Ticino

Welcome to Ticino, a beautiful area located in the southern part of Switzerland. Known for its Mediterranean climate, stunning lakes, charming towns, and rich Italian influence, Ticino offers a unique mix of Swiss efficiency and Italian charm. Here's an overview of what meets you in Ticino:

**Lugano**:
Start your exploration of Ticino in Lugano, the region's biggest city and cultural hub.
Stroll along the beautiful lakefront promenade of Lake Lugano, lined with cafes, restaurants, and boutique

shops.

Visit the historic Old Town (Città Vecchia) with its narrow cobblestone streets, charming parks, and Renaissance buildings.

Explore the splendid Parco Ciani, a scenic lakeside park with lush gardens, elegant houses, and peaceful walking paths.

Don't miss the chance to take a boat cruise on Lake Lugano and enjoy the breathtaking views of the surrounding mountains.

**Locarno**:

Travel to Locarno, a charming town set on the northern shore of Lake Maggiore.

Explore the historic Piazza Grande, known for its annual film festival and lined with bars, shops, and medieval arcades.

Visit the beautiful Old Town (Città Vecchia) with its colorful houses and winding streets.

Take a cable car ride to Cardada-Cimetta, where you can enjoy panoramic views of Lake Maggiore and the nearby mountains.

Don't miss the beautiful botanical gardens of the Brissago Islands, a short boat ride away from Locarno.

**Bellinzona**:

Discover Bellinzona, the city of Ticino and a UNESCO World Heritage Site.

Explore the ancient castles of Bellinzona, including Castelgrande, Montebello, and Sasso Corbaro.

Visit the Old Town (Centro Storico) with its charming streets, historic buildings, and lively markets.

Take a walk along the city walls, which offer panoramic views of the nearby landscapes.

Immerse yourself in the rich history and culture of the area at the Bellinzona Museums.

**Outdoor Activities**:

Ticino is a paradise for outdoor enthusiasts, offering a wide range of activities amid its beautiful natural landscapes.

Hike in the stunning valleys of Valle Verzasca, Valle Maggia, or Valle di Muggio.

Discover the scenic beauty of the Swiss National Park, located in the Graubünden area.

Enjoy water sports on the lakes of Lugano, Maggiore, or Como, such as swimming, sailing, or paddleboarding.

Relax on the lovely beaches and soak up the Mediterranean sunshine.

**Culinary Delights**:

Ticino is famous for its delicious cuisine, influenced by both Swiss and Italian traditions.

Indulge in local favorites such as risotto, polenta, gorgonzola cheese, and hearty stews.

Pair your meal with a glass of Merlot wine, made in the region's vineyards.

Don't forget to taste the famous Ticino chocolate, known for its high quality and rich flavors.

Ticino offers a captivating blend of natural beauty, cultural richness, and a relaxed Mediterranean environment. Whether you're exploring the lakeside towns, hiking in the mountains, or indulging in the local cuisine, Ticino is sure to leave you with unforgettable memories of your Swiss trip.

# A. Lugano

Welcome to Lugano, the biggest city in Ticino and a true gem in southern Switzerland. Known for its stunning location on Lake Lugano, charming old town, and Mediterranean flair, Lugano offers a delightful mix of natural beauty, cultural experiences, and Italian influence. Here's a full guide to help you make the most of your visit to Lugano:

**Lake Lugano and Promenade**:
Start your tour by taking a leisurely stroll along the scenic lakefront promenade of Lake Lugano.
Admire the crystal-clear waters of the lake and the nearby mountains.
Relax on one of the public beaches or enjoy a picnic in the beautifully designed parks.
Take a boat tour to explore the lake and enjoy panoramic views from the water.

**Old Town (Città Vecchia)**:

Immerse yourself in the charm of Lugano's Old Town, with its narrow cobblestone streets and ancient buildings. Visit the Piazza della Riforma, the main square of Lugano, surrounded by cafes, shops, and beautiful buildings.

Explore the Via Nassa, a busy pedestrian street known for its high-end boutiques, jewelry stores, and artisan shops.

Discover the picturesque churches and squares spread throughout the Old Town.

**Cultural Attractions**:

Visit the Lugano Cathedral (Cattedrale di San Lorenzo), a beautiful Renaissance-style cathedral with stunning frescoes and statues.

Explore the Museum of Art (Museo d'Arte della Svizzera Italiana) to admire a collection of modern and current art.

Discover the Hermann Hesse Museum, dedicated to the famous German-Swiss writer and Nobel laureate.

Don't miss the Cantonal Art Museum (Museo Cantonale d'Arte), showcasing works by local and foreign artists.

**Monte San Salvatore**:

Take a train ride up Monte San Salvatore, a mountain overlooking Lugano.

Enjoy panoramic views of Lake Lugano, the cityscape, and the surrounding Alps from the top.

Take a leisurely hike along the mountain trails or simply relax in the peaceful settings.

### Parco Ciani:
Visit Parco Ciani, a beautiful lakeside park that offers a tranquil escape from the bustling city.

Explore the lush gardens, fragrant flower beds, and picturesque paths.

Relax by the lake, rent a paddleboat, or enjoy a picnic in this quiet setting.

### Shopping and Dining:
Lugano is a paradise for shoppers, having a wide range of boutiques, designer stores, and Swiss watch shops.

Explore the Via Nassa and the nearby streets for luxury brands, jewelry, fashion, and Swiss chocolates.

Indulge in the culinary wonders of Lugano at the numerous restaurants, cafes, and gelaterias.

Try classic Ticinese dishes, such as risotto, polenta, and local cheeses, accompanied by regional wines.

### Lugano Cultural Events:
Lugano hosts different cultural events throughout the year, including music festivals, art exhibitions, and outdoor concerts.

Don't miss the Lugano Estival Jazz, a renowned jazz festival that attracts foreign artists every summer.

Check the local event calendar to see if there are any

cultural or music events going during your visit.

Lugano's blend of Swiss efficiency and Italian charm, coupled with its stunning lake views and cultural attractions, make it an enchanting location. Enjoy the beauty of Lugano and indulge in its rich culture and culinary offerings. Your time in Lugano is sure to be a unique experience.

## B. Locarno

Welcome to Locarno, a charming town set on the northern shore of Lake Maggiore in Ticino, Switzerland. Known for its mild temperature, beautiful landscapes, and rich cultural heritage, Locarno offers a delightful mix of history, natural beauty, and a relaxed Mediterranean atmosphere. Here's a full guide to help you make the most of your visit to Locarno:

### Piazza Grande:

Start your tour in Locarno's main square, Piazza Grande, known for its picturesque setting and vibrant atmosphere.

Admire the charming medieval alleys, elegant buildings, and the historic Town Hall (Palazzo Municipale).

Visit the weekly local market held in the square, where you can find fresh fruit, regional specialties, and artisan crafts.

**Old Town (Città Vecchia):**
Immerse yourself in the small winding streets and historic buildings of Locarno's Old Town.
Discover the medieval churches, charming squares, and secret corners filled with local shops and cafes.
Visit the Church of San Francesco, known for its beautiful paintings, and the Church of Santa Maria Assunta.

**Castello Visconteo:**
Explore the Castello Visconteo, a medieval castle that holds the Archaeological Museum of Locarno.
Learn about the history and archaeology of the area through the museum's exhibits.
Enjoy sweeping views of the town and Lake Maggiore from the castle's tower.

**Cardada-Cimetta:**
Take a cable car ride to Cardada-Cimetta, a high peak near Locarno.
Enjoy breathtaking views of Lake Maggiore, the surrounding mountains, and the charming towns below.
Explore the hiking trails and enjoy the tranquility of the alpine scenery.

**Madonna del Sasso:**
Visit the Sanctuary of the Madonna del Sasso, set on a hill overlooking Locarno.

Explore the beautiful church and enjoy panoramic views of the town, Lake Maggiore, and the nearby valleys.

Learn about the history and importance of the sanctuary, which is an important pilgrimage site.

**Ascona**:

Take a short trip from Locarno to the nearby town of Ascona, often referred to as the "Pearl of Lake Maggiore."

Explore the lovely lakeside promenade, lined with cafes, shops, and art galleries.

Wander through the small streets of the Old Town, with its colorful houses and Mediterranean ambiance.

Visit the Collegio Papio, a former convent that now holds an art collection and a botanical garden.

**Lake Maggiore**:

Enjoy the beauty of Lake Maggiore, one of the biggest and most scenic lakes in Switzerland.

Take a boat tour to explore the lake and visit the charming islands of Brissago, known for their botanical gardens.

Relax on the lakeside beaches, go for a swim, or participate in watersports like sailing, paddleboarding, or kayaking.

**Film Festival and Cultural Events**:

Locarno is famous for its annual Locarno Film Festival,

held in August, which draws filmmakers and cinema enthusiasts from around the world.
Check if there are any cultural events, concerts, or exhibitions going during your visit, as Locarno is known for its lively cultural scene.

Locarno's unique blend of Swiss efficiency and Mediterranean charm, coupled with its scenic beauty and cultural attractions, make it a captivating location. Enjoy the laid-back ambiance, discover the historic streets, and soak in the beauty of Lake Maggiore. Your time in Locarno is sure tobe a unique experience.

## C. Bellinzona

Welcome to Bellinzona, the city of Ticino and a UNESCO World Heritage Site. Known for its stunning medieval castles, charming old town, and rich history, Bellinzona offers a unique blend of cultural tradition and natural beauty. Here's a full guide to help you make the most of your visit to Bellinzona:

### Castles of Bellinzona:
Explore the three impressive medieval castles of Bellinzona: Castelgrande, Montebello, and Sasso Corbaro.
Start with Castelgrande, the biggest and most famous of the castles, which sits on a hill overlooking the city.

Visit the castle's museum to learn about its past and enjoy panoramic views of Bellinzona and the surrounding area.

Explore Montebello Castle, located on a nearby hill, known for its well-preserved defenses and beautiful views.

Lastly, visit Sasso Corbaro Castle, perched on a rocky outcrop, giving breathtaking vistas and a fascinating glimpse into the past.

**Old Town (Centro Storico):**

Immerse yourself in the lovely atmosphere of Bellinzona's Old Town.

Wander through the narrow streets, admire the well-preserved buildings, and find hidden squares and courtyards.

Visit the Piazza Collegiata, the main square, where you'll find the Collegiata Church with its beautiful paintings.

Explore the local shops, boutiques, and artisan workshops, and taste some delicious Ticinese cuisine at the cozy restaurants.

**Bellinzona Museums:**

Discover the rich cultural history of Bellinzona at its museums.

Visit the Museum Villa dei Cedri, which focuses on the history, art, and culture of the area.

Explore the Museum Castello di Montebello, located

within the castle, showing archaeological finds and historical artifacts.

Learn about the unique culture and customs of Ticino at the Museo Etnografico Ticinese.

**Rabadan Carnival:**

If you're visiting Bellinzona in February, don't miss the Rabadan Carnival, one of the biggest and most colorful carnival celebrations in Switzerland.

Join the festivities, admire the colorful costumes, and enjoy the lively parades and music performances.

**Bellinzona Market:**

Experience the lively atmosphere of the Bellinzona Market, held every Saturday in the city center.

Explore the stalls filled with fresh local food, regional specialties, artisan crafts, and clothes.

Sample delicious cheeses, salted meats, and freshly baked bread while immersing yourself in the local culture.

**Outdoor Activities:**

Bellinzona is surrounded by beautiful natural scenery, offering opportunities for outdoor adventures.

Take a leisurely hike in the nearby valleys, such as the Valle Verzasca or Valle Maggia, and find picturesque landscapes.

Enjoy cycling along the scenic bike paths that meander

through the Ticino area.

If you're looking for more adrenaline, try rock climbing or canyoning in the stunning gorges and cliffs of the area.

**Bellinzona Festivals and Events**:

Throughout the year, Bellinzona hosts different festivals and events that celebrate local traditions, music, and cuisine.

Check the local event calendar to see if there are any cultural events, music concerts, or food festivals going during your visit.

Bellinzona's medieval castles, picturesque old town, and vibrant cultural scene make it a captivating location. Immerse yourself in the history, explore the castles, savor the local flavors, and enjoy the natural beauty of the nearby landscapes. Your time in Bellinzona is sure to be a memorable experience.

## 5.7 Valais

Welcome to Valais, a picturesque area in southern Switzerland known for its majestic mountains, charming Alpine villages, and world-class ski resorts. Valais offers a stunning natural scenery, rich cultural heritage, and a wide range of outdoor activities. Here's an overview of what meets you in Valais:

**Matterhorn**:

One of the most iconic peaks in the Swiss Alps, the Matterhorn is a must-see sight in Valais.

Marvel at its pyramid-like shape and enjoy panoramic views from viewpoints in Zermatt or nearby areas.

Consider taking a cable car ride to Gornergrat for a closer view of the Matterhorn and the nearby Alpine scenery.

**Ski Resorts**:

Valais is home to some of the best ski resorts in the world, drawing winter sports enthusiasts from around the globe.

Zermatt, Verbier, Saas-Fee, and Crans-Montana are famous for their excellent slopes, stunning vistas, and vibrant après-ski scenes.

Enjoy a wide range of winter sports, including skiing, snowboarding, snowshoeing, and ice climbing.

**Thermal Baths and Wellness**:

Valais boasts several thermal baths and wellness centers where you can relax and refresh.

Leukerbad, famous for its natural hot springs, offers a range of spa facilities and outdoor thermal pools.

Other wellness places in Valais include Brigerbad, Ovronnaz, and Bagnes, giving a blissful retreat for relaxation.

**Wine and Vineyards**:

Valais is Switzerland's largest wine-growing region, known for its vineyards and exceptional wines.

Explore the vineyards of Sion, Sierre, and Martigny, and

delight in wine tasting at local wineries.

Sample unique grape varieties, such as Petite Arvine and Cornalin, and learn the region's winemaking traditions.

**Aletsch Glacier**:

Visit the Aletsch Glacier, the biggest glacier in the Alps and a UNESCO World Heritage Site.

Take a guided hike or cable car ride to discover the glacier's awe-inspiring ice formations and breathtaking landscapes.

Enjoy panoramic views from locations like Bettmerhorn and Eggishorn.

**Sion**:

Discover the vibrant city of Sion, the capital of Valais, known for its rich history and cultural assets.

Explore the charming Old Town, with its narrow streets, medieval houses, and the towering Sion Castle.

Visit the Museum of Valais, which displays the region's history, art, and traditions.

**Hiking and Outdoor Adventures**:

Valais is a paradise for outdoor enthusiasts, offering countless hiking trails, mountain biking routes, and climbing possibilities.

Explore the scenic trails of the UNESCO-protected Jungfrau-Aletsch area or hike along the famous Europaweg trail.

Engage in adrenaline-pumping sports like paragliding, canyoning, and via ferrata.

**Swiss Cuisine**:

Valais is renowned for its delicious local cuisine, which includes hearty mountain dishes and regional specialties.

Indulge in raclette, fondue, dried meat (viande des Grisons), and traditional Valaisian rye bread.

Pair your meal with a glass of Valais wine for a complete dining experience.

Valais offers a perfect mix of natural beauty, adventure, relaxation, and cultural experiences. Whether you're exploring the stunning mountain peaks, enjoying winter sports, relaxing in thermal baths, or savoring local delicacies, Valais is sure to leave you with unforgettable memories of your Swiss trip.

## A. Zermatt

Welcome to Zermatt, a world-renowned Alpine resort town set in the Swiss Alps. Known for its breathtaking mountain scenery, including the famous Matterhorn, Zermatt offers a perfect blend of natural beauty, outdoor adventures, and Swiss charm. Here's a very detailed guide to help you make the most of your visit to Zermatt:

### Matterhorn:
The Matterhorn is Zermatt's most iconic landmark and a must-see destination.

Marvel at its distinctive pyramid shape and majestic presence as it towers over the town.

Enjoy panoramic views of the Matterhorn from different viewpoints in Zermatt, such as Gornergrat or Sunnegga.

Consider taking a cable car ride to the Matterhorn Glacier Paradise, the highest cable car stop in Europe, for incredible vistas.

**Skiing and Snowboarding**:

Zermatt is a world-class ski resort, offering exceptional slopes for skiers and snowboarders of all types.

Explore the vast network of ski runs, including the Matterhorn Glacier, Schwarzsee, and Gornergrat areas.

Enjoy reliable snow conditions, stunning Alpine scenery, and access to nearby Italian ski resorts through the Matterhorn Glacier Paradise.

**Gornergrat Railway**:

Take a scenic train ride on the Gornergrat Railway, one of Switzerland's most famous mountain lines.

Enjoy stunning views of the surrounding peaks, glaciers, and valleys as the train ascends to the Gornergrat summit.

Visit the observation platform at Gornergrat to catch unforgettable photos of the Matterhorn and the Monte Rosa massif.

**Hiking and Mountain Climbing**:

Zermatt offers an extensive network of hiking trails, ranging from leisurely walks to challenging mountain treks.

Explore the flower-filled meadows, tranquil valleys, and dramatic peaks as you hike through the nearby landscapes.

For experienced climbers, there are chances to conquer famous peaks like the Breithorn or the Matterhorn under the guidance of certified mountain guides.

**Glacier Paradise**:

Visit the Matterhorn Glacier Paradise, situated at an altitude of 3,883 meters (12,740 feet).

Explore the ice palace, a stunning world of ice sculptures and caves within the glacier.

Take in panoramic views from the viewing deck and enjoy a meal at Europe's highest-altitude restaurant.

**Alpine Lakes**:

Discover the picturesque mountain lakes near Zermatt, such as Stellisee and Schwarzsee.

Take a leisurely walk around the lakes, admire the mirror-like reflections of the nearby peaks, and enjoy the peaceful ambiance.

**Zermatt Village**:

Explore the car-free town of Zermatt with its charming streets, traditional chalets, and cozy mountain atmosphere.

Stroll along the Bahnhofstrasse, the main street lined

with boutiques, bars, and Swiss chocolate shops.

Visit the local museums, such as the Matterhorn Museum or the Zermatlantis, to learn about the history and culture of the area.

Swiss Cuisine:

Indulge in traditional Swiss food at Zermatt's many restaurants and mountain huts.

Treat yourself to Swiss cheese fondue, raclette, rösti (potato dish), and hearty Alpine favorites.

Pair your meal with a glass of local Valais wine or enjoy Swiss chocolate for dessert.

Zermatt offers a unique Alpine experience with its stunning scenery, world-class skiing, and a range of outdoor activities. Whether you're exploring the Matterhorn, skiing the slopes, hiking the trails, or indulging in Swiss cuisine and culture, Zermatt is sure to provide you with an amazing Swiss adventure.

## B Saas-Fee Guide

Welcome to Saas-Fee, a picturesque Alpine town nestled in the Swiss Alps. Known as the "Pearl of the Alps," Saas-Fee offers a tranquil escape surrounded by majestic hills, pristine glaciers, and a car-free environment. Here's a full guide to help you make the most of your visit to Saas-Fee:

**Skiing and Snowboarding**:

Saas-Fee is a renowned ski resort, having excellent slopes for skiers and snowboarders of all levels.

Enjoy the vast ski area with its well-groomed pistes, freeride opportunities, and terrain parks.

Take advantage of the high-altitude position to enjoy reliable snow conditions throughout the season.

**Hiking and Mountaineering**:

Saas-Fee is a paradise for hiking enthusiasts, with numerous well-marked tracks catering to all levels of fitness and experience.

Explore the breathtaking scenery, alpine meadows, and gorgeous viewpoints as you hike through the Saas Valley.

For more adventurous mountaineers, there are chances to climb the surrounding peaks or take guided glacier treks.

**Feeblitz and Felskinn**:

Enjoy an exciting ride on the Feeblitz, an Alpine roller coaster that winds through the mountainside.

Take the Felskinn cable car to reach the mountain station and enjoy panoramic views of the nearby peaks.

Discover the revolving restaurant and the observation platform offering breathtaking views of the Saas Valley.

**Hannig Mountain**:

Take a gondola ride to Hannig Mountain, giving a peaceful retreat and stunning views.

Explore the themed hiking trails, visit the marmot viewing point, or relax at the mountain restaurant.

**Saas-Fee Village**:

Explore the charming car-free town of Saas-Fee with its narrow streets, wooden houses, and alpine ambiance.

Stroll along the busy main street, lined with shops, boutiques, and cozy cafés.

Visit the local museum to learn about the history, culture, and customs of Saas-Fee and its surrounding area.

**Adventure Sports**:

Experience adrenaline-pumping sports in Saas-Fee, such as paragliding, ice climbing, or via ferrata.

Test your skills at the outdoor climbing park or go mountain biking on the trails that crisscross the area.

Wellness and Relaxation:

Indulge in wellness and relaxation at the local spa and fitness centers.

Enjoy a soothing massage, soak in hot thermal baths, or relax in saunas and steam rooms.

Swiss Cuisine:

Savor the flavors of Swiss food at Saas-Fee's restaurants and mountain huts.

Delight in traditional dishes like raclette, fondue, or Swiss rosti, made with locally sourced ingredients.

Treat yourself to Swiss chocolate or taste regional specialties like Saaser Älplermagronen (Swiss macaroni dish) or Saaser Roggenbrot (rye bread).

Saas-Fee offers a perfect mix of natural beauty, outdoor adventures, and a serene Alpine atmosphere. Whether you're skiing the slopes, hiking the trails, or indulging in Swiss hospitality and food, Saas-Fee is sure to provide you with an unforgettable

## C. Verbier

Welcome to Verbier, a world-renowned Alpine town located in the Val de Bagnes in southwestern Switzerland. Known for its stunning mountain scenery, extensive ski slopes, and lively après-ski scene, Verbier offers a perfect blend of outdoor adventures and luxurious amenities. Here's a full guide to help you make the most of your visit to Verbier:

**Skiing and Snowboarding**:

Verbier is part of the expansive 4 Vallées ski area, having over 400 kilometers of ski slopes for all levels of skiers and snowboarders.

Enjoy a range of terrain, from gentle beginner slopes to challenging off-piste areas and mogul runs.

Take advantage of the extensive lift system and visit the neighboring resorts of Nendaz, Veysonnaz, and Thyon.

**Off-Piste and Freeride**:

Verbier is known for its exceptional off-piste and freeride opportunities.

Engage in exciting adventures with a qualified guide and discover the backcountry areas, such as the famous itinerary runs and the legendary Mont Fort.

**Mont Fort**:

Take the cable car to the top of Mont Fort, the highest point in the 4 Vallées ski area.

Marvel at the sweeping views of the surrounding Alpine peaks, including the Matterhorn, Mont Blanc, and the Grand Combin.

Enjoy the exciting descents from Mont Fort, suitable for advanced skiers and snowboarders.

**Verbier Village**:

Explore the charming town of Verbier with its traditional chalets, expensive hotels, and bustling atmosphere.

Stroll along the lively Rue de Médran, lined with boutique shops, sports stores, and trendy après-ski bars.

Visit the local market to try regional products and traditional Swiss delicacies.

**Verbier Festival**:

If you're coming during the summer, don't miss the Verbier Festival, a world-renowned classical music event.

Enjoy performances by widely famous musicians and attend masterclasses and open rehearsals.

**Hiking and Mountain Biking**:

During the summer months, Verbier offers a plethora of hiking and mountain bike trails.

Explore the pristine alpine scenery, follow the well-marked trails, and enjoy the breathtaking views.

Take a cable car or chairlift to reach higher elevations and discover panoramic viewpoints.

**Verbier Xtreme**:

If you're a fan of extreme sports, visit Verbier during the Verbier Xtreme, an annual freeride challenge.

Watch the world's top skiers and snowboarders showcase their skills on the difficult slopes of the Bec des Rosses.

**Wellness and Relaxation**:

Indulge in health and relaxation at the local spas and wellness centers in Verbier.

Unwind in saunas, steam rooms, and Jacuzzis, or treat yourself to a rejuvenating massage or beauty service.

**Dining and Après-Ski**:

Verbier offers a lively après-ski scene with numerous bars and restaurants catering to all tastes.

Enjoy a cozy après-ski drink at one of the mountain huts or indulge in gourmet food at the village's upscale restaurants.

Try classic Swiss dishes like fondue, raclette, or rösti, accompanied by a glass of local Swiss wine.

Verbier's combination of world-class skiing, stunning mountain scenery, and lively social scene make it a premier location for outdoor enthusiasts and those wanting an active and luxurious getaway. Whether you're hitting the slopes, enjoying the après-ski, or exploring the mountain trails, Verbier offers a truly unforgettable experience.

## 5.8 Graubünden

Welcome to Graubünden, Switzerland's biggest canton, located in the eastern part of the country. Known for its majestic mountains, charming villages, and rich cultural history, Graubünden offers a diverse range of attractions and activities. Here's an overview of what meets you in Graubünden:

**Majestic Mountain Peaks**:
Graubünden is home to several famous mountain areas, including the stunning peaks of the Swiss Alps.
Explore the majestic Piz Bernina, the highest peak entirely within Switzerland, or face the challenging Piz Palü.
Enjoy panoramic views of the surrounding mountains, glaciers, and rivers as you hike or take scenic cable car rides.

**Ski Resorts**:
Graubünden boasts numerous world-class ski resorts, making it a popular location for winter sports enthusiasts.
Experience the vast ski areas of St. Moritz, Davos, Arosa, Lenzerheide, or Flims-Laax.
Enjoy a wide range of skiing and snowboarding options, from gentle slopes for beginners to challenging runs for experts.

**Engadin Valley**:
Explore the picturesque Engadin Valley, known for its pristine alpine scenery, turquoise lakes, and charming towns.
Visit St. Moritz, a glamorous resort town famous for its expensive hotels, high-end shopping, and winter sports

events.

Discover the charming village of Sils-Maria, where famous writer Friedrich Nietzsche found inspiration for his works.

**Glacier Express**:

Embark on a scenic train trip aboard the Glacier Express, one of Switzerland's most famous panoramic trains.

Marvel at the stunning views as the train winds through Graubünden, passing over impressive viaducts and through picturesque valleys.

Admire the UNESCO World Heritage-listed Albula and Bernina train lines, which form part of the Glacier Express route.

**Swiss National Park**:

Explore the Swiss National Park, nestled in the heart of Graubünden.

Embark on hiking trails that wind through the park, allowing you to find its diverse flora and fauna.

Observe native wildlife, including ibex, chamois, marmots, and a range of bird species.

**Historic Towns and Architecture**:

Graubünden is home to several historic towns and villages that showcase its rich architectural history.

Explore the charming old town of Chur, the canton's center, with its well-preserved medieval buildings.

Visit the scenic town of Guarda, known for its beautifully kept Engadine houses and traditional architecture.

**Culinary Delights**:

Graubünden is known for its unique cuisine, which blends Swiss, Italian, and Austrian influences.

Try traditional meals like capuns (chard rolls), pizzoccheri (buckwheat pasta with vegetables and cheese), and maluns (grated potato dish).

Sample local favorites such as Bündner Nusstorte (nut tart) and Bündnerfleisch (dried meat).

**Outdoor Activities**:

Graubünden offers a wide range of outdoor sports beyond skiing, including hiking, mountain biking, and rock climbing.

Explore the extensive network of hiking trails that crisscross the area, offering breathtaking views and diverse landscapes.

Enjoy water sports on the region's lakes, such as windsurfing, paddleboarding, or sailing.

Graubünden's combination of natural beauty, rich history, and outdoor adventures make it a captivating location. Whether you're discovering its majestic mountain peaks, indulging in its culinary delights, or immersingyourself in its charming towns, Graubünden promises a memorable experience.

## A. Davos

Welcome to Davos, a picturesque town nestled in the Swiss Alps and known as one of the world's most famous winter sports destinations. With its stunning mountain landscapes, world-class ski resorts, and lively cultural scene, Davos offers a perfect blend of outdoor adventures, relaxation, and entertainment. Here's a very detailed guide to help you make the most of your visit to **Davos**:

Skiing and Snowboarding:

Davos is part of the vast Davos Klosters ski area, having over 300 kilometers of ski slopes for all levels of skiers and snowboarders.

Enjoy a range of terrain, from gentle beginner slopes to challenging black runs and thrilling freestyle parks.

Take advantage of the efficient lift system, including funiculars, cable cars, and chairlifts, to explore the entire ski area.

**Parsenn**:

Discover the Parsenn ski area, one of the most famous sections of Davos Klosters.

Enjoy long and wide slopes perfect for intermediate and advanced skiers.

Take the Parsenn funicular and cable cars to reach the highest point and enjoy amazing panoramic views.

**Jakobshorn**:

Visit Jakobshorn, a favorite among freestyle fans and adrenaline seekers.

Explore the Jakobshorn snow park, equipped with jumps, rails, and halfpipes for snowboarders and freestyle skiers.

Experience the famous Jakobshorn JatzPark, a playground for snowboarders with various challenges and jumps.

**Cross-Country Skiing**:

Davos boasts an extensive network of cross-country skiing trails, reaching over 100 kilometers.

Glide through picturesque valleys, snowy woods, and frozen lakes, enjoying the tranquility of the surrounding nature.

Take part in cross-country skiing lessons or join guided tours to discover the most beautiful tracks.

**Winter Hiking and Snowshoeing**:

Explore the winter paradise of Davos on foot through the well-marked winter hiking trails.

Enjoy peaceful walks amidst snow-covered scenery, frozen waterfalls, and breathtaking views.

Try snowshoeing, a popular activity that allows you to travel off the beaten path and explore remote areas.

**Cultural Highlights**:

Davos is renowned for its vibrant culture scene, hosting numerous events, festivals, and art exhibitions throughout the year.

Visit the Kirchner Museum, dedicated to the works of Ernst Ludwig Kirchner and other modern artists.

Attend the annual Spengler Cup, an international ice hockey tournament that draws teams from around the world.

**Wellness and Relaxation**:

After an exhilarating day on the slopes, indulge in rest at Davos' wellness centers and spas.

Enjoy saunas, steam baths, hot tubs, and different wellness treatments to rejuvenate your body and mind.

Take advantage of the healing qualities of the region's fresh mountain air and mineral-rich thermal waters.

**Davos Lake**:

During the winter, Davos Lake transforms into a natural ice rink, giving ice skating and ice hockey opportunities.

Rent skates and glide across the frozen lake while enjoying the beautiful surroundings.

Join a game of ice hockey or watch local teams fight in thrilling matches.

**Culinary Delights**:

Davos offers a diverse food scene with a wide range of restaurants and bars to suit all tastes.

Sample classic Swiss cuisine, including fondue, raclette, and hearty mountain specialties.

Explore foreign flavors, from Italian and Asian to gourmet fine dining experiences.

**Davos Congress Center**:

Davos is also famous for hosting the World EconomicForum at the Davos Congress Center. While it's not directly related to tourism, it's worth mentioning the significance of this annual event that brings together global leaders, politicians, and business figures to discuss pressing economic and social problems.

**Summer Activities**:

In the summer months, Davos offers a wide range of outdoor activities such as hiking, mountain biking, and skiing.

Explore the network of hiking trails that lead to breathtaking views, alpine meadows, and crystal-clear mountain lakes.

Enjoy mountain biking on the well-marked tracks or take part in the annual Swiss Epic mountain bike race.

**Schatzalp**:

Take a nostalgic trip to Schatzalp, a stunning alpine resort available by a funicular ride from Davos.

Explore the beautiful botanical gardens and enjoy panoramic views of Davos from the mountain's deck.

Visit the historic Schatzalp Hotel, known as the inspiration for Thomas Mann's book "The Magic Mountain."

Davos offers a perfect mix of thrilling outdoor adventures, cultural experiences, and relaxation opportunities. Whether you're hitting the slopes, immersing yourself in the lively arts scene, or indulging in Swiss cuisine, Davos is sure to provide you with an unforgettable Swiss Alpine experience.

## B. St. Moritz

Welcome to St. Moritz, one of the world's most prestigious Alpine resorts and a symbol of wealth, elegance, and winter sports excellence. Nestled in the Engadin Valley in the Swiss canton of Graubünden, St. Moritz offers a unique mix of breathtaking natural beauty, glamorous attractions, and a rich cultural heritage. Here's a very thorough guide to help you make the most of your visit to St. Moritz:

**Skiing and Snowboarding**:

St. Moritz is renowned for its exceptional skiing and snowboarding possibilities.

Explore the vast ski area of the Upper Engadin, which includes four main ski areas: Corviglia, Corvatsch, Diavolezza, and Zuoz.

Enjoy a wide range of ski slopes catering to all levels, from gentle beginning runs to challenging black pistes.

Take advantage of the great snow conditions, state-of-the-art lifts, and stunning panoramic views.

**Cresta Run**:

Experience the thrill of the Cresta Run, a world-famous natural ice skeleton track.

Take part in a thrilling ride down the icy track, hitting speeds of up to 130 kilometers per hour.

Join the St. Moritz Tobogganing Club for an unforgettable journey and a chance to become part of a storied tradition.

**St. Moritz Lake**:

Discover the frozen beauty of St. Moritz Lake during the winter months.

Engage in ice skating, curling, or a game of ice hockey

on the natural ice rink.

Witness exciting events like the White Turf horse races, which take place on the frozen lake.

### Segantini Museum:

Visit the Segantini Museum, dedicated to the works of Giovanni Segantini, one of the most important Alpine painters.

Explore the museum's collection of Segantini's stunning landscape paintings, showcasing the beauty of the Engadin area.

### Engadine Museum:

Immerse yourself in the rich history and culture of the Engadin area at the Engadine Museum.

Learn about the traditional culture, architecture, and crafts of the local population.

Discover the fascinating stories of St. Moritz's growth as a world-class resort.

### Muottas Muragl:

Take a thrilling ride on the funicular to Muottas Muragl, a mountain offering panoramic views of the Engadin Valley.

Enjoy stunning views of the surrounding peaks, lakes, and charming Engadin villages.

Go for a leisurely walk or snowshoeing adventure on the well-marked trails and experience the tranquility of the Alpine scenery.

### Winter Hiking:

St. Moritz and its surroundings offer a plethora of winter

hiking tracks.

Explore the scenic routes that wind through snow-covered woods, along frozen lakes, and across peaceful meadows.

Enjoy the crisp mountain air, spectacular views, and the chance to spot local wildlife.

**Gourmet Cuisine**:

Indulge in St. Moritz's exceptional culinary scene, having a wide range of gourmet restaurants and cozy mountain huts.

Sample classic Swiss specialties like fondue, raclette, and Engadin nut cake.

Discover innovative dishes made by world-class chefs using locally sourced products.

**Wellness and Relaxation**:

St. Moritz is home to numerous luxury spas and wellness centers, great for relaxation and rejuvenation.

Treat yourself to a range of wellness treatments, including massages, facials, and thermal baths.

Enjoy the healing qualities of the region's natural mineral-rich springs and serene surroundings.

**Polo Matches**:

Witness the exciting sport of polo at the St. Moritz Polo World Cup on Snow.

Watch world-class polo players fight on the frozen lake, creating a unique and captivating spectacle.

Engadin Skimarathon:

If you're visiting in early March, enjoy the Engadin

Skimarathon, one of the largest cross-country ski races in the world.

Take part in the marathon or cheer on the participants as they cross the scenic Engadin Valley.

**Shopping**:

St. Moritz is a paradise for luxury shopping fans.

Explore the exclusive boutiques, jewelry stores, and high-end fashion brands along Via Serlas, St. Moritz's famous shopping street.

Discover unique Swiss watches, designer clothing, and luxurious goods from foreign names.

St. Moritz offers a unique mix of glamour, outdoor adventures, cultural experiences, and relaxation. Whether you're hitting the slopes, immersing yourself in the arts and culture, or indulging in culinary delights, St. Moritz offers a truly memorable Swiss Alpine experience.

## C. Arosa

Welcome to Arosa, a charming mountain town nestled in the Swiss Alps and known for its idyllic setting, pristine nature, and wide range of outdoor activities. Located in the canton of Graubünden, Arosa offers a perfect mix of natural beauty, recreational opportunities, and a peaceful alpine ambiance. Here's a full guide to help you make the most of your visit to Arosa:

**Skiing and Snowboarding**:

Arosa is a popular ski resort, having a variety of slopes suitable for all levels of skiers and snowboarders.

Explore the Arosa Lenzerheide ski area, which boasts over 225 kilometers of ski runs and modern lift services.

Enjoy a range of terrain, from gentle beginning slopes to challenging black runs and off-piste areas.

**Weisshorn**:

Take the cable car to the top of Weisshorn, one of the main peaks in the Arosa Lenzerheide ski area.

Marvel at the panoramic views of the surrounding mountains, valleys, and the picturesque Arosa town.

Enjoy thrilling descents down the mountain or start on a snowshoeing adventure through the pristine winter landscapes.

**Tschuggen Grand Hotel**:

Visit the iconic Tschuggen Grand Hotel, a renowned luxury hotel known for its distinctive design.

Admire the hotel's unique Tschuggen Bergoase spa, created by architect Mario Botta, offering relaxation and wellness facilities.

Enjoy a meal at one of the hotel's exceptional restaurants or indulge in a luxurious spa service.

**Ice Skating and Curling**:

Engage in ice skating or try your hand at curling at the Arosa Ice Rink.

Enjoy a fun-filled day gliding across the ice, surrounded by the stunning mountain scenery.

Rent skates on-site or bring your own for a memorable ice skating adventure.

**Winter Hiking and Snowshoeing**:

Arosa offers a network of well-marked winter hiking tracks and snowshoeing routes.

Explore the peaceful snowy landscapes, forests, and frozen lakes as you journey through the winter wonderland.

Rent snowshoes or join guided snowshoeing tours to find the hidden corners of Arosa.

**Bergkirchli**:

Visit Bergkirchli, a small mountain church perched on a rocky outcrop above Arosa.

Take a short hike to reach the chapel and enjoy panoramic views of Arosa and the nearby mountains.

Explore the neighboring exhibition about the region's past and cultural heritage.

**Arosa Bärenland**:

Visit Arosa Bärenland, a sanctuary for rescued bears found in the nearby mountains.

Learn about bear conservation and observe the bears in their natural habitat, having a safe and protected environment.

**Culinary Delights**:

Arosa offers a variety of dining choices, ranging from cozy mountain huts to gourmet restaurants.

Enjoy traditional Swiss food, including cheese fondue, raclette, and hearty regional dishes.

Sample local favorites like Arosa honey or Aroser cake, a delicious treat made with local ingredients.

**Music and Cultural Events**:

Arosa hosts different music and cultural events throughout the year.

Attend concerts, festivals, or art exhibitions that feature local and foreign talents.

Immerse yourself in the vibrant culture scene and experience the unique atmosphere of Arosa's artistic community.

**Relaxation and Wellness**:

Arosa is a perfect destination for relaxation and health.

Unwind and refresh in one of the local spas, offering a range of treatments and therapies.

Enjoy a soothing massage, rest in saunas and steam rooms, or take a dip in thermal baths.

Take advantage of the tranquil mountain settings and fresh alpine air for a truly rejuvenating experience.

Arosa's natural beauty, recreational activities, and peaceful atmosphere make it an ideal destination for those wanting a tranquil Alpine getaway. Whether you're hitting the slopes, exploring the winter trails, or indulging in relaxation and culinary delights, Arosa offers a memorable Swiss Alpine experience.

# Top Attractions and Landmarks

## 6.1 Matterhorn

Welcome to the majestic Matterhorn, one of the world's most famous mountains and a symbol of Switzerland's natural beauty. Located in the Pennine Alps, the Matterhorn offers a breathtaking backdrop with its unique pyramid shape and towering presence. Here's a very thorough guide to help you make the most of your visit to the Matterhorn:

**Overview**:
The Matterhorn stands at an impressive height of 4,478 meters (14,692 feet) and is one of the highest hills in the Alps.
Its symmetrical shape and imposing presence have made

it a favorite subject for artists, photographers, and mountaineers alike.

The mountain straddles the border between Switzerland and Italy, with the Swiss side being more available for visitors.

## Zermatt:

Zermatt, a charming Alpine town located at the foot of the Matterhorn, serves as the main gateway to the mountain.

Explore the car-free streets of Zermatt, filled with classic Swiss chalets, shops, restaurants, and cozy cafes.

Enjoy the enchanting atmosphere and take in the breathtaking views of the Matterhorn from different vantage points in the village.

## The Matterhorn Experience:

Take a cable car or cogwheel train to reach the different viewpoints around the Matterhorn.

The Gornergrat Railway offers a scenic journey to the Gornergrat top, where you can enjoy stunning panoramic views of the Matterhorn and the surrounding peaks.

Visit the Matterhorn Glacier Paradise, accessed by the highest cable car station in Europe, and experience breathtaking vistas from its viewing deck.

## Hiking and Mountaineering:

The Matterhorn is a magnet for mountaineers and hiking

fans from around the world.

Experienced climbers can start on the challenging ascent of the Matterhorn's summit, known for its technical difficulty and demanding conditions.

For hikers, there are several trails that lead to viewpoints giving incredible views of the Matterhorn, such as the Five Lakes Trail or the Riffelsee Trail.

## The Matterhorn Museum:

In Zermatt, visit the Matterhorn Museum to learn about the history, geology, and mountaineering heritage of the area.

Discover the stories of the first ascents, the impact of tourists on Zermatt, and the legends surrounding the mountain.

Explore the exhibits showing mountaineering gear, artifacts, and pictures that tell the captivating story of the Matterhorn.

## Skiing and Snowboarding:

Zermatt offers world-class skiing and snowboarding possibilities with its extensive ski area, including the Matterhorn Glacier Paradise.

Enjoy a range of slopes catering to all levels, from gentle beginner runs to challenging off-piste terrain.

Take in the stunning alpine scenery as you carve your way down the slopes, with the Matterhorn as your background.

**Photography and Sightseeing**:

The Matterhorn is a photographer's paradise, offering countless chances for capturing stunning images.

Explore various viewpoints and vantage points around Zermatt to capture the Matterhorn from different angles and in different lighting situations.

Don't miss the iconic image of the Matterhorn in the tranquil waters of the Riffelsee or Stellisee lakes during sunrise or sunset.

**Dining and Après-Ski**:

Indulge in delicious Swiss cuisine and foreign dishes at the restaurants and mountain huts in Zermatt.

After a day of outdoor activities, unwind with après-ski drinks and live music at the lively bars and lounges in the town.

Try traditional Swiss dishes like cheese fondue or raclette, and taste themouthwatering flavors while enjoying the mountain ambiance.

Safety and Precautions:

When visiting the Matterhorn, it's important to prioritize safety and be aware of the mountain's challenging nature.

If you plan to climb the Matterhorn, ensure you have proper mountaineering experience, equipment, and information.

Follow the advice of local guides and adhere to safety

rules to minimize risks and ensure a safe and enjoyable experience.

**Weather Considerations**:
The weather conditions around the Matterhorn can change quickly, so it's crucial to stay informed and check the forecast.
Dress in layers, wear appropriate outdoor gear, and carry basics like sunscreen, a hat, and sufficient water.
Keep in mind that certain activities, such as climbing or reaching higher viewpoints, may be subject to weather restrictions or closures.

The Matterhorn is an awe-inspiring natural wonder that captivates tourists with its beauty and grandeur. Whether you choose to admire it from the picturesque village of Zermatt, take on a mountaineering adventure, or capture its magnificence through photography, the Matterhorn offers an unforgettable experience that will leave you in awe of nature's marvels.

## 6.2 Château de Chillon

Welcome to the Château de Chillon, an enchanting castle set on the shores of Lake Geneva in Switzerland. With its rich history, stunning architecture, and picturesque setting, the Château de Chillon is a must-visit site for history enthusiasts and lovers of medieval architecture.

Here's a full guide to help you make the most of your visit to the Château de Chillon:

**History and Architecture**:
The Château de Chillon goes back over 1,000 years and is considered one of the most well-preserved medieval castles in Switzerland.
Explore the castle's various architectural styles, running from medieval fortress structures to Renaissance and Gothic elements.
Admire the well-preserved towers, courtyards, dungeons, and living rooms that provide a glimpse into the castle's storied past.

**Guided Tours**:
Take advantage of the guided tours offered at the Château de Chillon to fully immerse yourself in its history and tales.
Knowledgeable guides will share fascinating stories about the castle's inhabitants, including the Counts of Savoy and important figures like Lord Byron.
Learn about the castle's strategic location, its role in trade routes, and its importance in Swiss history.

**The Great Halls and Living Quarters**:
Step into the magnificent Great Halls, which were once used for important receptions and banquets.
Marvel at the grandeur of the rooms, adorned with

detailed tapestries, decorative frescoes, and period furniture.

Explore the living quarters and imagine what life was like for the castle's inhabitants throughout the ages.

### The Chapel:

Visit the castle's chapel, an intimate place with beautiful stained glass windows and ornate decorations.

Experience the peaceful ambiance of this sacred place and respect the artistry and craftsmanship displayed within.

### The Courtyards and Gardens:

Wander through the castle's courtyards, giving stunning views of Lake Geneva and the surrounding mountains.

Admire the well-maintained grounds, where you can relax and enjoy the serene atmosphere.

Capture memorable pictures of the castle's exterior from different vantage points.

### The Underground Dungeons:

Descend into the castle's underground cells, which once served as prisons.

Explore the dark and mysterious passageways, finding the chilling stories associated with the castle's prisoners and their conditions.

Admire the intricate carvings and inscriptions left behind by the prisoners, giving a haunting glimpse into their lives.

**Cultural Events and Exhibitions**:
The Château de Chillon hosts different cultural events, exhibitions, and concerts throughout the year.
Check the castle's schedule to see if any special events align with your visit, such as medieval reenactments or art displays.
Immerse yourself in the lively cultural scene and experience the castle in a unique and dynamic way.

**Lake Geneva Views and Surroundings**:
Take a moment to enjoy the stunning views of Lake Geneva and the Swiss Alps from the castle's vantage points.
Consider taking a leisurely stroll along the lake promenade or having a picnic in the nearby park.
Combine your visit to the Château de Chillon with a boat trip on Lake Geneva to further explore the region's beauty.

The Château de Chillon offers a fascinating trip through time, allowing you to explore centuries of history within its walls. With its architectural splendor, captivating stories, and stunning surroundings, a visit to the Château de Chillon is sure to leave you with lasting memories and a deeper respect for Switzerland's cultural heritage and medieval past. Enjoy your exploration of this remarkable castle and the enchanting Lake Geneva area.

## 6.3 Lake Geneva

Welcome to Lake Geneva, one of Switzerland's most iconic and picturesque locations. Located on the border between Switzerland and France, Lake Geneva, also known as Lac Léman, offers a harmonious mix of natural beauty, cultural treasures, and recreational activities. Here's a full guide to help you make the most of your visit to Lake Geneva:

**Overview**:
Lake Geneva is the biggest lake in Switzerland, spanning approximately 580 square kilometers (224 square miles). It is renowned for its crystal-clear waters, surrounded by breathtaking scenery, vineyards, and charming towns.
The lake's shores are divided between Switzerland and France, with famous destinations including Geneva, Lausanne, Montreux, and Evian-les-Bains.

**Geneva**:
Start your Lake Geneva trip in the vibrant city of Geneva, known for its cosmopolitan atmosphere, historic landmarks, and diplomatic importance.
Explore the charming Old Town, visit famous sites like Jet d'Eau and St. Pierre Cathedral, and enjoy the city's cultural diversity.

**Lausanne**:
Continue your trip to Lausanne, a lively city perched on

the hills overlooking Lake Geneva.

Visit the Olympic Museum, explore the picturesque Old Town, and take in panoramic views from the church tower.

Stroll along the lake promenade and enjoy the lively café culture and waterfront ambiance.

## Montreux:

Experience the charm of Montreux, a town famous for its annual Montreux Jazz Festival and stunning lakeside setting.

Explore the Chillon Castle, a medieval castle perched on a rocky outcrop near Montreux.

Enjoy a leisurely walk along the Montreux Promenade, lined with beautiful flowers, sculptures, and stunning lake views.

## Vevey:

Visit Vevey, a picturesque town known for its connection with the famous Swiss chocolate brand, Nestlé.

Explore the Chaplin's World museum, dedicated to the life and works of the famous comedian Charlie Chaplin.

Take a relaxing walk along the lakeside promenade, adorned with charming cafes, boutiques, and art works.

## Evian-les-Bains:

Cross the border into France and visit the elegant town of Evian-les-Bains, known for its mineral water and luxurious spa resorts.

Discover the source of Evian mineral water, visit the Cachat Spring Pavilion, and learn about the town's rich history.

Relax in the lakeside parks, enjoy a boat ride on the lake, or indulge in wellness treatments at the famous spas.

**Vineyards and Wine Tasting**:

Lake Geneva's shores are dotted with vineyards that make exceptional wines.

Take a wine tour and visit local wineries to taste exquisite Swiss wines, including Chasselas, the region's flagship grape variety.

Learn about the winemaking process, enjoy panoramic views of the vineyards, and savor the flavors of the area.

**Outdoor Activities**:

Lake Geneva offers a wide range of outdoor activities for nature lovers.

Take a boat cruise on the lake to enjoy the stunning scenery and explore different lakeside towns.

Engage in water sports such as paddleboarding, sailing, or kayaking.

Hike or bike along the lake's picturesque trails, allowing you to immerse yourself in the natural beauty of the area.

**Lakeside Cuisine**:

Lake Geneva is renowned for its culinary delights, blending Swiss, French, and foreign influences.

Indulge in fresh seafood, lake fish, and local favorites such as fondue, raclette, and Swiss chocolate.
Visitone of the waterfront restaurants or lakeside cafes to savor delicious meals while enjoying the panoramic lake views.

### Festivals and Events:
Lake Geneva hosts a range of festivals and events throughout the year.
Attend the Montreux Jazz Festival, which draws renowned musicians from around the world.
Experience the Fête de l'Escalade in Geneva, a lively celebration of the city's historical win.
Check the local event calendars for concerts, cultural exhibitions, and traditional festivities during your stay.

### Relaxation and Wellness:
Lake Geneva is a haven for relaxation and health.
Treat yourself to a spa day at one of the luxury resorts along the lake, indulging in rejuvenating treatments and thermal pools.
Find tranquility in lakeside parks and gardens, where you can unwind, meditate, or simply enjoy the peaceful settings.
Lake Geneva offers a perfect mix of natural beauty, cultural treasures, and recreational activities. Whether you're exploring the charming lakeside towns, indulging in culinary delights, or immersing yourself in the lake's

tranquil ambiance, Lake Geneva promises an unforgettable experience that will leave you with cherished memories of your Swiss-French Alpine holiday.

## 6.4 The Rhine Falls

Welcome to the Rhine Falls, the biggest waterfall in Europe and a natural wonder located in northern Switzerland. Situated near the town of Schaffhausen, the Rhine Falls captivates tourists with its sheer power, breathtaking beauty, and immersive surroundings. Here's a full guide to help you make the most of your visit to the Rhine Falls:

**Overview**:
The Rhine Falls is made by the majestic Rhine River as it cascades down a series of rocks and makes a magnificent spectacle.
With a width of 150 meters (492 feet) and a height of 23 meters (75 feet), the Rhine Falls is an awe-inspiring natural wonder.

**Observation Decks**:
Begin your visit by heading to the different observation decks strategically positioned for the best views of the falls.
The platforms offer panoramic views of the cascading

water, allowing you to appreciate the power and grandeur of the Rhine Falls up close.

**Boat Tours**:

Enhance your experience by taking a boat tour that gets you closer to the falls.

Hop aboard one of the excursion boats available and cruise along the Rhine River, getting a unique view of the falls from the water.

Feel the mist on your face as you approach the falls and wonder at their imposing presence.

**Adventure Activities**:

For those seeking an adrenaline rush, the Rhine Falls offers exciting adventure sports.

Try the "Rhine Falls Adventure Park" located near the falls, where you can participate in thrilling experiences such as zip-lining, rock climbing, and rope courses.

These activities provide a unique chance to explore the surrounding natural landscapes and enjoy an exhilarating adventure.

**Hiking Trails**:

Embark on one of the hiking trails around the Rhine Falls to further absorb yourself in the beauty of the area.

Follow the well-marked paths that wind through lush forests, giving scenic views of the falls and the surrounding landscape.

Discover secret viewpoints and enjoy peaceful moments in nature as you explore the trails at your own pace.

**Visitor Center and Exhibitions**:
Visit the Rhine Falls Visitor Center to learn more about the history, geology, and environment of the falls.
Explore the interactive exhibits and displays that provide insights into the formation and importance of the Rhine Falls.
Gain a better understanding of the natural processes and the cultural heritage associated with this remarkable natural attraction.

**Picnic Areas and Restaurants**:
Take advantage of the marked picnic areas near the falls to enjoy a leisurely meal amidst stunning surroundings.
Alternatively, choose one of the restaurants or cafes overlooking the falls to taste a delicious meal while taking in the breathtaking views.
Indulge in local Swiss cuisine or foreign dishes while surrounded by the beauty of the Rhine Falls.

**Surrounding Attractions**:
Explore the charming town of Schaffhausen, located nearby, and walk through its picturesque streets lined with historical buildings and shops.
Visit the medieval fortress of Munot, giving panoramic views of Schaffhausen and the Rhine River.

Discover the nearby Rhine River Valley, with its vineyards, castles, and charming villages, giving additional chances for exploration.

The Rhine Falls offers a captivating experience that combines the raw power of nature with breathtaking beauty. Whether you're admiring the falls from the viewing decks, taking a boat tour, engaging in adventure activities, or simply enjoying a picnic in the scenic surroundings, the Rhine Falls promises a memorable visit and a deep appreciation for the wonders of the natural world.

## 6.5 The Aletsch Glacier

Welcome to the Aletsch Glacier, a beautiful natural wonder and a UNESCO World Heritage site located in the Swiss Alps. Stretching over 23 kilometers (14 miles) in length, the Aletsch Glacier is the largest glacier in the Alps and an awe-inspiring sight to view. Here's a full guide to help you make the most of your visit to the Aletsch Glacier:

**Overview**:

The Aletsch Glacier is set in the Jungfrau-Aletsch-Bietschhorn region, which is known for its breathtaking alpine landscapes.

Comprised of millions of tons of ice, the glacier is a wonder of nature and a testament to the power of glacial erosion.

**Jungfraujoch**:
Begin your trip to the Aletsch Glacier by heading to Jungfraujoch, often referred to as the "Top of Europe."

Take a scenic train ride to Jungfraujoch, which is the highest railway station in Europe, and enjoy panoramic views of the nearby mountains.

From Jungfraujoch, you can access different viewpoints and hiking trails that offer stunning vistas of the glacier.

Aletsch Arena:
Explore the Aletsch Arena, a region containing the Aletsch Glacier and its surrounding area.

Engage in a range of outdoor activities, including hiking, skiing, and snowshoeing, depending on the season.

Follow the designated trails that provide access to viewpoints giving breathtaking views of the glacier and the surrounding Alpine scenery.

**Aletsch Glacier Panorama Trail**:
Embark on the Aletsch Glacier Panorama Trail, a well-marked hiking route that provides a close-up view of the glacier.

Enjoy a leisurely walk along the path, taking in the awe-inspiring views of the massive ice formations, crevasses, and rugged mountain peaks.

Marvel at the blue glacial meltwater lakes that dot the landscape, creating a stunning contrast against the ice.

**Great Aletsch Forest**:

Discover the Great Aletsch Forest, a pristine and protected area near the Aletsch Glacier.

Immerse yourself in the tranquility of the forest as you walk along the marked trails, surrounded by towering trees and lush vegetation.

Keep an eye out for local wildlife, such as ibex, chamois, and different bird species that call this area home.

Jungfraufirn Viewpoint:

Visit the Jungfraufirn Viewpoint, a vantage place that offers a spectacular view of the Aletsch Glacier and its glacial tributaries.

From this elevated position, you can enjoy the vastness of the glacier and the intricate network of ice formations that extend into the distance.

Take time to absorb the serenity and grandeur of the glacier, capturing unforgettable memories through photos.

**Guided Glacier Tours**:

Consider joining a guided glacier tour to gain a deeper knowledge of the Aletsch Glacier's formation, movement, and significance.

Accompanied by knowledgeable guides, you'll learn about glaciology, the effects of climate change, and the unique ecosystem surrounding the glacier.

Engage in educational events that provide insight into

the glacier's importance in the region's ecological balance.

**Environmental Conservation**:
The Aletsch Glacier and its surrounding area are carefully preserved to keep their natural beauty and ecological balance.
Follow designated paths and respect the marked limits to minimize your impact on the fragile environment.
Take note of any guidelines or restrictions in place to ensure the long-term preservation of this amazing natural treasure.
Visiting the Aletsch Glacier offers a remarkable chance to witness the raw power and beauty of nature. Whether you're exploring the glacier on foot, admiring it from panoramic viewpoints, or learning about its ecological importance, the Aletsch Glacier promises an unforgettable experience that will leave you with a deep appreciation for the wonders of the natural world.

## 6.6 Swiss National Park Guide

Welcome to the Swiss National Park, a pristine wilderness set in the heart of the Alps and Switzerland's oldest national park. Spanning over 170 square kilometers (65 square miles), the Swiss National Park is a haven for nature lovers, offering unspoiled landscapes, diverse wildlife, and countless opportunities for outdoor adventure. Here's a full guide to help you make the most of your visit to the Swiss National Park:

**Overview**:
The Swiss National Park was created in 1914 and is dedicated to the conservation of natural habitats, flora, and fauna.

It is home to a wide range of Alpine ecosystems, including dense woods, meadows, rocky slopes, and snow-capped peaks.

The park's main objective is to preserve its pristine wilderness and allow visitors to experience nature in its purest form.

**Hiking Trails**:
Explore the network of well-marked hiking trails that crisscross the park, giving stunning views and encounters with wildlife.

Follow the designated paths that range from easy walks to more challenging hikes, catering to different fitness levels and hobbies.

Immerse yourself in the tranquil surroundings as you cross forests, meadows, and alpine landscapes.

**Wildlife Watching**:
The Swiss National Park is renowned for its rich biodiversity and the chance to observe native wildlife.

Keep an eye out for ibex, chamois, marmots, red deer,

and a range of bird species as you explore the park.

Respect the park's regulations and keep a safe distance to observe the animals in their natural habitat without disturbing them.

### Visitor Center:

Start your visit at the Swiss National Park Visitor Center, where you can receive park information, maps, and guidebooks.

Learn about the park's past, flora, fauna, and ongoing conservation efforts through interactive exhibits and educational displays.

Attend presentations or take guided walks led by knowledgeable park staff to gain deeper insights into the park's ecosystems.

### Picnic Areas and Facilities:

Take advantage of the marked picnic areas within the park to enjoy a leisurely meal surrounded by nature.

Many of these places offer breathtaking views of the surrounding mountains, valleys, and alpine meadows.

Restrooms and other facilities are available at different locations within the park for visitors' convenience.

Photography and Nature Observation:

Capture the park's natural beauty and wildlife through photography, but remember to protect the environment and wildlife.

Use long lenses to watch and photograph animals from a

safe distance without causing disturbance.

Take time to enjoy the small wonders of nature, such as wildflowers, insect life, and the changing colors of the seasons.

**Environmental Conservation**:

The Swiss National Park puts a strong emphasis on environmental conservation and sustainability.

Stay on designated trails to protect fragile ecosystems and avoid soil erosion.

Follow the park's guidelines regarding waste management and minimize your effect on the natural surroundings.

**Accommodation and Camping**:

While camping is not allowed within the park, there are accommodation options in the surrounding areas.

Consider stopping in nearby towns or villages and plan day trips to explore the Swiss National Park.

Ensure that you respect the park's regulations and guidelines when coming from external accommodations.

The Swiss National Park provides a unique opportunity to immerse yourself in pristine nature, observe Alpine ecosystems, and meet diverse wildlife. As you explore the park's hiking trails, observe the animals, and enjoy the untouched landscapes, you will gain a deep respect for the importance of conservation and the delicate balance of our natural world.

## 6.7 The Lauterbrunnen Valley

Welcome to the Lauterbrunnen Valley, a picturesque and captivating spot nestled in the Swiss Alps. Known as the "Valley of Waterfalls," Lauterbrunnen Valley is famous for its stunning natural beauty, towering cliffs, verdant fields, and cascading waterfalls. Here's a full guide to help you make the most of your visit to the Lauterbrunnen Valley:

**Overview**:
The Lauterbrunnen Valley is located in the Bernese Oberland region of Switzerland, surrounded by majestic mountains and Alpine scenery.
The valley runs for 4 kilometers (2.5 miles) and is named after the Lauterbrunnen River, which flows through it.
The valley's charm lies in its idyllic setting, with charming towns, lush green fields, and over 70 magnificent waterfalls.

**Waterfalls**:
Marvel at the amazing waterfalls that adorn the Lauterbrunnen Valley, creating a dramatic and awe-inspiring ambiance.
Visit famous waterfalls such as the Staubbach Falls, which cascades over a 297-meter (974-foot) cliff, creating a mesmerizing spectacle.
Explore other gorgeous falls like the Trümmelbach Falls,

a series of powerful cascades hidden within a mountain gorge.

**Hiking and Nature Walks**:
The Lauterbrunnen Valley offers an extensive network of hiking trails and nature walks, allowing you to experience its natural wonders.
Embark on the scenic Lauterbrunnen Valley Loop Trail, which takes you through charming towns, past waterfalls, and into the heart of the valley.
Discover the panoramic views from vantage points like Grütschalp or Mürren, offering breathtaking vistas of the nearby mountains and valleys.

**Village Exploration**:
Take time to discover the charming villages that dot the Lauterbrunnen Valley, each with its own unique character and charm.
Visit Lauterbrunnen, the main town, with its traditional Swiss architecture, quaint shops, and welcoming cafes.
Explore other villages like Wengen, Mürren, and Stechelberg, each giving its own unique atmosphere and stunning views of the surrounding peaks.

**Adventure Sports**:
For adrenaline fans, the Lauterbrunnen Valley offers a range of adventure sports and outdoor activities.
Engage in paragliding, where you can soar through the

sky and experience breathtaking aerial views of the valley and nearby mountains.

Try canyoning, rock climbing, or mountain biking, taking advantage of the valley's rugged scenery and natural features.

**Cable Cars and Funiculars**:

Utilize the efficient cable car and funicular system in the Lauterbrunnen Valley to reach higher viewpoints and explore the surrounding mountains.

Take the cable car to Schilthorn or the funicular to the Allmendhubel viewpoint for panoramic views of the valley and the famous Eiger, Mönch, and Jungfrau mountains.

**Local Cuisine and Cafes**:

Indulge in the local food and traditional Swiss delicacies at the charming restaurants and cafes in the Lauterbrunnen Valley.

Treat yourself to Swiss cheese fondue, rösti (a Swiss potato dish), or try local dishes made with Alpine ingredients.

Take a moment to rest and enjoy a cup of Swiss coffee or hot chocolate while soaking in the tranquil alpine atmosphere.

**Winter Activities**:

In winter, the Lauterbrunnen Valley transformsinto a

winter wonderland, offering a range of activities for snow lovers.

Hit the slopes at nearby ski resorts such as Mürren-Schilthorn or Wengen-Grindelwald, known for their various ski runs and breathtaking alpine scenery.

Engage in snowshoeing or winter hiking to discover the snow-covered landscapes and enjoy the calm of the valley in its winter attire.

**Cultural Experiences**:

Immerse yourself in the local culture and customs of the Lauterbrunnen Valley.

Attend festivals and events that celebrate Swiss folklore, music, and cuisine, giving insights into the rich heritage of the region.

Visit local museums and exhibitions to learn about the valley's history, alpine farming methods, and traditional crafts.

**Nature Conservation**:

The Lauterbrunnen Valley is a protected natural area, and it's important to respect its fragile ecosystems and wildlife.

Stick to marked paths and trails, ensuring you do not disturb the flora and fauna.

Follow the principles of Leave No Trace, disposing of waste properly and leaving the natural world as you found it.

The Lauterbrunnen Valley offers a captivating mix of natural beauty, outdoor adventures, and traditional Swiss charm. Whether you're mesmerized by the cascading waterfalls, exploring the hiking trails, or immersing yourself in the local culture, the Lauterbrunnen Valley offers a memorable and enriching experience in the heart of the Swiss Alps.

## 6.8 Zermatt and the Gornergrat Railway

Welcome to Zermatt, a world-renowned mountain town nestled in the Swiss Alps and home to the iconic Matterhorn. Known for its stunning alpine beauty, picturesque streets, and excellent outdoor opportunities, Zermatt is a paradise for nature fans and adventure seekers. One of the must-visit sites in Zermatt is the Gornergrat Railway, offering breathtaking views of the surrounding peaks. Here's a full guide to help you make the most of your visit to Zermatt and the Gornergrat Railway:

**Overview of Zermatt**:
Zermatt is a car-free village situated at the foot of the Matterhorn, one of the most famous mountains in the world.
Wander through the charming streets lined with traditional Swiss houses, boutique shops, and cozy

restaurants.

Enjoy the stunning alpine scenery, with towering peaks, lush fields, and crystal-clear streams.

**The Matterhorn**:

Marvel at the majestic Matterhorn, an iconic mountain that stands tall and commands the Zermatt skyline.

Capture unforgettable photos of this famous peak, especially during sunrise or sunset when the colors are at their most dramatic.

Consider taking a cable car or cogwheel train to get closer to the Matterhorn and enjoy panoramic views from higher spots.

**Gornergrat Railway**:

Hop aboard the Gornergrat Railway, a historic cogwheel train that takes you on a scenic trip to the summit of Gornergrat.

The Gornergrat Railway gives stunning views of the surrounding peaks, including the Matterhorn, Monte Rosa, and the Gorner Glacier.

Enjoy the comfortable ride as the train climbs through alpine landscapes, passing charming mountain towns and alpine meadows.

**Gornergrat Summit**:

Arriving at the Gornergrat summit, you'll be greeted with awe-inspiring views that run as far as the eye can see.

Take in the panoramic views of the surrounding 29 peaks that soar above 4,000 meters (13,000 feet).

Visit the viewing platform for an unobstructed view of the Matterhorn and the nearby alpine panorama.

### Hiking and Exploring:

Embark on one of the many hiking trails around the Gornergrat peak to immerse yourself in the alpine beauty.

Choose from easy walks to difficult hikes, allowing you to explore the alpine flora, enjoy the fresh mountain air, and experience the tranquility of the high peaks.

Discover the Gornergrat Glacier, which is available from the summit and offers a fascinating glimpse into the world of glaciers.

### Alpine Wildlife:

Keep an eye out for mountain wildlife during your visit to Zermatt and the Gornergrat Railway.

Spot marmots, chamois, and golden eagles as you explore the hillside.

Join a guided wildlife tour to learn more about the unique fauna and their responses to the alpine environment.

### Alpine Cuisine and Après-Ski:

After a day of exploration, indulge in the delicious alpine food offered in Zermatt's restaurants and mountain huts.

Sample classic Swiss meals such as fondue, raclette, or hearty alpine stews.

Enjoy a well-deserved après-ski drink in one of the cozy mountain bars, taking in the alpine atmosphere.

**Outdoor Activities**:

Zermatt is a playground for outdoor lovers, offering a wide range of activities for all seasons.

In winter, hit the hills and enjoy skiing, snowboarding, or cross-country skiing on the world-class pistes.

In summer, explore the hiking and mountain biking trails, go rock climbing, or try paragliding for an exhilarating aerial view.

Engage in other activities such as climbing, glacier trekking, or even heli-skiing for a truly adventurous experience.

**Alpine Wellness and Relaxation**:

Treat yourself to some well-deserved rest and rejuvenation in Zermatt's wellness centers and spas.

Unwind in hot baths, enjoy a massage, or take part in yoga or meditation classes.

Take advantage of the tranquil alpine settings to find peace and serenity amidst the stunning natural landscapes.

**Sustainability and Nature Conservation**:

Zermatt has a strong commitment to sustainability and

saving its natural environment.

Support eco-friendly practices by following the ideals of Leave No Trace, disposing of waste properly, and respecting wildlife and vegetation.

Explore Zermatt's efforts in renewable energy, electric transportation, and environmentally conscious practices.

Zermatt and the Gornergrat Railway offer an unforgettable alpine experience, mixing breathtaking natural beauty, thrilling adventures, and Swiss hospitality. Whether you're capturing the essence of the Matterhorn, taking the Gornergrat Railway to the top, or exploring the countless outdoor activities, Zermatt promises a memorable trip into the heart of the Swiss Alps.

## 6.9 The Bernese Oberland Railway Guide

Welcome to the Bernese Oberland Railway, a scenic railway trip through the spectacular landscapes of the Bernese Oberland region in Switzerland. This railway network connects some of the most beautiful and picturesque places, offering breathtaking views of towering mountains, shimmering lakes, and charming alpine towns. Here's a full guide to help you make the most of your journey on the Bernese Oberland Railway:

**Overview**:

The Bernese Oberland Railway is a network of train

lines that cross the Bernese Oberland region in Switzerland.

The railway ride takes you through stunning alpine scenery, including snow-capped peaks, deep valleys, and pristine lakes.

This route is known for its panoramic vistas, offering unparalleled views of famous Swiss landmarks.

Interlaken:

Begin your journey in Interlaken, a famous tourist hub and the gateway to the Bernese Oberland region.

Explore the charming town, with its lovely shops, restaurants, and proximity to two beautiful lakes, Lake Thun and Lake Brienz.

From Interlaken, you can access different train routes that will take you deeper into the Bernese Oberland.

### Jungfraujoch:

Embark on the famous Jungfraujoch Railway, also known as the "Top of Europe" trip.

This railway takes you to the highest railway station in Europe, located at an elevation of 3,454 meters (11,332 feet) amidst the Jungfrau mountain range.

Enjoy breathtaking views of glaciers, snow-covered peaks, and the awe-inspiring Aletsch Glacier, the biggest glacier in the Alps.

### Lauterbrunnen Valley:

Explore the beautiful Lauterbrunnen Valley, often

referred to as the "Valley of Waterfalls."

Take a train from Interlaken to Lauterbrunnen, a charming town nestled in the valley, surrounded by towering cliffs and cascading waterfalls.

From Lauterbrunnen, you can continue your journey to Wengen or Grindelwald, two alpine resorts offering stunning mountain views.

**Wengen**:

Board the Wengernalp Railway, a cogwheel train that takes you from Lauterbrunnen to the car-free town of Wengen.

Enjoy the traditional alpine atmosphere, charming chalets, and panoramic views of the surrounding mountains, including the famous Eiger, Mönch, and Jungfrau peaks.

Wengen is a good base for outdoor activities such as hiking, skiing, and exploring the nearby Kleine Scheidegg area.

**Grindelwald**:

Alternatively, take the train from Lauterbrunnen to Grindelwald, another enchanting alpine village in the Bernese Oberland.

Known as the "Eiger Village," Grindelwald gives access to numerous hiking trails, ski slopes, and adventure activities.

Enjoy the stunning views of the Eiger North Face and

the nearby alpine landscapes.

**Lake Thun and Lake Brienz**:
Experience the beauty of the region's lakes by taking a boat ride on Lake Thun or Lake Brienz.
The turquoise waters against the setting of the snow-capped mountains create a mesmerizing scene.
Explore charming lakeside towns like Thun or Brienz, where you can stroll along the promenades, visit museums, or take a leisurely swim.

**Scenic Routes and Panoramic Trains**:
Along the Bernese Oberland Railway, you'll have the chance to experience several scenic routes and panoramic train rides.
**The GoldenPass Line**: This panoramic train route connects Lucerne to Interlaken, passing through picturesque landscapes, charming villages, and giving stunning views of lakes and mountains.
The Glacier Express: While not part of the Bernese Oberland Railway, the Glacier Express is an iconic train trip that connects Zermatt to St. Moritz. It traverses the Swiss Alps, including the Bernese Oberland region, offering breathtaking views of alpine scenery.

**Hiking and Outdoor Activities**:
The Bernese Oberland area is a paradise for outdoor enthusiasts, with numerous hiking trails and outdoor

activities.

Explore the well-marked trails that lead you through alpine meadows, lush woods, and breathtaking mountain passes.

Engage in sports such as mountain biking, paragliding, or even skiing and snowboarding during the winter months.

**Alpine Cuisine and Local Delicacies**:

Along the Bernese Oberland Railway, you'll have the chance to savor delicious Swiss cuisine and local specialties.

Try traditional dishes such as cheese fondue, raclette, or rosti, followed by Swiss chocolates or a refreshing glass of local beer or wine.

Don't miss the chance to taste regional delicacies like Berner Platte or Bernese-style Alpine cheeses.

**Sustainability and Nature Conservation**:

The Bernese Oberland region prides itself on its commitment to sustainability and nature conservation.

Follow responsible travel practices, such as staying on marked trails, disposing of waste properly, and respecting wildlife and vegetation.

Support eco-friendly initiatives and local businesses that value sustainability and environmental preservation.

The Bernese Oberland Railway offers a remarkable journey through the breathtaking landscapes of the Swiss

Alps. Whether you're admiring panoramic vistas from the train, exploring alpine villages, embarking on outdoor adventures, or savoring local cuisine, this railway journey promises an unforgettable experience filled with natural beauty and Swiss charm.

## 6.10 The Golden Pass Route

Welcome to the Golden Pass Route, a scenic railway journey that takes you through some of the most beautiful landscapes in Switzerland. The Golden Pass Route is renowned for its picturesque vistas, charming alpine villages, and cultural highlights. Here's a detailed guide to help you make the most of your journey on the Golden Pass Route:

**Overview**:
The Golden Pass Route is a panoramic train route that connects Lucerne to Lake Geneva, passing through the heart of Switzerland.
The route offers a diverse range of landscapes, including snow-capped mountains, serene lakes, rolling hills, and lush meadows.
The journey is divided into three sections: Lucerne to Interlaken, Interlaken to Zweisimmen, and Zweisimmen to Montreux.

**Lucerne**:

Start your journey in Lucerne, a picturesque city situated on the shores of Lake Lucerne.

Explore the charming Old Town, visit iconic landmarks such as the Chapel Bridge and the Lion Monument, and enjoy the vibrant atmosphere of the city.

From Lucerne, board the Golden Pass train and prepare to be mesmerized by the stunning scenery that awaits you.

**Interlaken**:

The first leg of the Golden Pass Route takes you from Lucerne to Interlaken, a popular tourist destination nestled between Lake Thun and Lake Brienz.

Admire the panoramic views of the surrounding mountains, including the iconic Eiger, Mönch, and Jungfrau peaks.

Explore the town's vibrant streets, indulge in adventure activities, or simply relax by the tranquil lakeside.

**Interlaken to Zweisimmen**:

The second leg of the journey takes you from Interlaken to Zweisimmen, crossing the beautiful Simmental Valley.

Marvel at the ever-changing landscapes as the train winds its way through lush meadows, quaint villages, and rolling hills.

Enjoy panoramic views of the Bernese Alps and soak in the peaceful ambiance of the Swiss countryside.

**Zweisimmen to Montreux**:

The final leg of the Golden Pass Route takes you from Zweisimmen to Montreux, situated on the shores of Lake Geneva.

Experience a change in scenery as you descend through the vineyards of the Lavaux region, a UNESCO World Heritage site.

Arrive in Montreux, known for its picturesque promenade, the Chillon Castle, and its annual jazz festival.

**Optional Side Trips**:

Along the Golden Pass Route, you have the option to embark on various side trips to explore additional highlights of the region.

Consider a visit to the Jungfraujoch, the "Top of Europe," or take a boat cruise on Lake Thun or Lake Brienz.

Explore the charming alpine villages of Gstaad or enjoy outdoor activities such as hiking or skiing, depending on the season.

**Cultural Highlights**:

The Golden Pass Route not only offers stunning natural scenery but also provides cultural highlights along the way.

Discover the rich heritage of Switzerland as you pass through traditional Swiss villages, historic towns, and cultural landmarks.

Immerse yourself in local traditions, sample regional cuisine, and learn about the history and customs of the Swiss people.

**Comfort and Amenities**:

The Golden Pass trains are known for their comfort and amenities, ensuring a pleasant journey.

Sit back in spacious seats, enjoy large panoramic windows for unobstructed views, and take advantage of onboard services.

Some trains even offer dining cars, allowing you to savor delicious meals while admiring the passing scenery.

**Sustainability and Nature Conservation**:

As you embark on the Golden Pass Route, it's important to embrace sustainable travel practices and respect the environment.

Dispose of waste responsibly and follow the principles of Leave No Trace.

Support local businesses and initiatives that prioritize sustainability and contribute to the preservation of the natural surroundings.

The Golden Pass Route offers a truly unforgettable railway journey through the stunning landscapes of Switzerland. From the vibrant city of Lucerne to the serene shores of Lake Geneva, this scenic route allows you to immerse yourself in the beauty of the Swiss Alps, experience local culture, and create lasting memories along the way. Enjoy the picturesque vistas, charming villages, and cultural highlights as you embark on this remarkable adventure through the heart of Switzerland.

# Outdoor Activities and Adventure

## 7.1 Hiking and Trekking

Switzerland is a paradise for hikers and outdoor enthusiasts, offering a vast network of hiking trails that cross breathtaking landscapes, from lush valleys to rugged mountain peaks. Whether you're a seasoned hiker or a beginner, there are hiking choices suitable for all fitness levels. Here's a guide to help you make the most of your hiking and trekking experiences in Switzerland:

**Trail Variety**:

Switzerland boasts a diverse range of hiking trails, catering to all tastes and abilities.

Explore well-marked trails that lead you through alpine meadows, dense woods, picturesque lakes, and towering hills.

Choose from easy and moderate routes for leisurely walks or push yourself with more demanding hikes that reward you with spectacular views.

**Iconic Hiking Trails**:

The Swiss Alps offer some of the most famous hiking trails in the world.

Consider hiking the Haute Route, a famous trek that takes you through high mountain passes and offers stunning views of the surrounding peaks.

Explore the Via Alpina, a long-distance hiking trail that spans across Switzerland, showing the country's diverse landscapes.

**Alpine Huts and Accommodation**:

Along popular hiking routes, you'll find a network of alpine huts and mountain refuges that provide lodging and meals for hikers.

Plan your walks in advance and consider booking a stay at these mountain huts to immerse yourself in the alpine experience.

Keep in mind that reservations might be needed during peak hiking seasons, so plan accordingly.

**Safety and Preparation**:
Before going on a hike, familiarize yourself with the trail, its difficulty level, and the expected duration.
Check the weather outlook and be prepared for changes in weather conditions, especially at higher altitudes.
Wear appropriate clothing and footwear, and carry necessary items such as a map, compass, first aid kit, extra layers, and adequate food and water.

**Mountain Guides and Tours**:
If you prefer a guided hiking experience or want to explore more challenging routes, try hiring a certified mountain guide.
Mountain guides offer expertise, local knowledge, and ensure your safety during more technical hikes or in remote places.
Joining organized hiking tours can also provide convenience and the chance to meet fellow hikers from around the world.

**Wildlife and Nature Observation**:
Switzerland's hiking trails often lead you through pristine natural environments, where you can meet a variety of wildlife and flora.
Keep a polite distance from wild animals and refrain from feeding or disturbing them.
Observe local laws and guidelines regarding protected areas and wildlife conservation.

**Hut-to-Hut Trekking**:

For a multi-day adventure, consider embarking on a hut-to-hut trekking journey.

Plan your route, book accommodations in advance, and hike from one alpine hut to another, visiting different regions and landscapes.

Hut-to-hut treks provide a unique chance to fully immerse yourself in the mountains, away from the hustle and bustle of daily life.

**Alpine Safety**:

If you plan to venture into higher alpine regions or try more challenging hikes, ensure you have the necessary skills and experience.

Familiarize yourself with alpine safety methods, including glacier travel, self-arrest, and navigation in steep terrain.

Consider taking mountaineering classes or hiring a guide for more technical hikes.

Switzerland's hiking and trekking opportunities are endless, giving something for everyone, from casual walkers to avid mountaineers. As you explore the country's scenic trails, take your time to enjoy the breathtaking landscapes, embrace the serenity of nature, and create unforgettable memories along theway. Remember to always prioritize safety, respect the environment, and adhere to local laws to ensure a memorable and responsible hiking experience in Switzerland.

## 7.2 Skiing and Snowboarding

Switzerland is renowned for its world-class ski resorts and offers excellent skiing and snowboarding options for enthusiasts of all levels. With its stunning alpine scenery, pristine slopes, and reliable snow conditions, Switzerland is a winter paradise. Here's a guide to help you make the most of your sledding and snowboarding adventures:

**Ski Resorts**:
Switzerland is home to numerous ski resorts, each having unique experiences and a range of slopes for all abilities.

Zermatt, located at the foot of the iconic Matterhorn, offers extensive slopes, stunning panoramic views, and a lively après-ski scene.

Verbier in the Four Valleys area is known for its challenging terrain and vibrant nightlife, attracting advanced skiers and snowboarders.

St. Moritz, a luxury resort in the Engadin Valley, offers a combination of glamorous ambiance and diverse skiing possibilities.

**Slope Variety**:

Switzerland's ski resorts cater to skiers and snowboarders of all kinds, from beginners to experts.

Choose resorts with specific beginner areas and gentle slopes if you're new to skiing or snowboarding.

Intermediate skiers can enjoy a wide range of well-groomed pistes, while advanced riders can face challenging black runs, moguls, and off-piste terrain.

**Off-Piste Skiing and Snowboarding**:

Switzerland's vast mountainous terrain offers exceptional chances for off-piste skiing and snowboarding.

Engage the services of a qualified mountain guide to discover pristine powder fields, hidden valleys, and thrilling descents.

Ensure you have the necessary avalanche safety equipment and understanding to venture into unmarked areas.

**Snowpark and Freestyle Facilities**:

Many Swiss ski resorts have specific snowparks and freestyle facilities for those interested in jumps, rails, and freestyle tricks.

Check out resorts like Laax, renowned for its world-class freestyle park with features suited for all skill levels.

Some resorts also offer snowboarding and skiing lessons especially tailored to freestyle enthusiasts.

**Ski Lessons**:

If you're new to skiing or snowboarding or want to improve your skills, consider taking lessons from skilled ski instructors.

Ski schools in Switzerland provide lessons for all ages and abilities, helping you gain confidence and improve your technique.

Private lessons are also offered for personalized guidance and faster progression.

**Cross-Country Skiing**:

Switzerland offers an extensive network of cross-country skiing trails, known as Nordic skiing.

Explore scenic scenery and serene winter wonderlands as you glide through groomed tracks.

Resorts like Engadin St. Moritz and Goms in the Valais region are popular for cross-country skiing.

**Après-Ski and Mountain Dining**:

After a day on the slopes, unwind and indulge in the famous Swiss après-ski culture.

Relax at cozy mountain huts, enjoy traditional alpine food, and savor a hot drink or a well-deserved après-ski beverage.

Resorts like Verbier, Zermatt, and St. Moritz offer a vibrant après-ski scene with bars, live music, and theater.

**Winter Activities**:

While skiing and snowboarding take center stage, Switzerland also offers a range of other winter activities. Try snowshoeing, ice skating, tobogganing, or take a scenic sleigh ride to enjoy the winter wonderland.

Some resorts even offer sports like ice climbing, ice karting, or helicopter skiing for an extra thrill.

**Equipment Rental and Services**:
Most ski areas have rental shops where you can hire ski or snowboard equipment if you don't have your own.

Ensure that your equipment is properly fitted and in good shape to ensure a safe and enjoyable experience.

Additionally, resorts offer services such as ski tuning, repairs, and storage facilities for your comfort.

**Safety and Mountain Etiquette**:
Prioritize safety on the slopes by following the rules and standards set by the resort.

Be aware of your skill level and choose slopes that fit your abilities.

Respect other skiers and snowboarders, giving them room and yielding to those downhill or in front of you.

Familiarize yourself with mountain safety protocols, including avalanche awareness and proper behavior in alpine environments.

Switzerland's ski resorts provide a winter playground for skiing and snowboarding fans. With a variety of slopes, stunning mountain scenery, and a range of winter activities, Switzerland offers an unforgettable winter sports experience. So strap on your skis or snowboard, hit the slopes, and immerse yourself in the thrill of Switzerland's snowy beauty

## 7.3 Mountain Biking

Switzerland offers incredible opportunities for mountain biking, with its diverse landscapes, well-maintained trails, and breathtaking mountain views. Whether you're a beginner or an experienced rider, Switzerland has trails to fit all skill levels. Here's a guide to help you make the most of your mountain bike adventures:

**Trail Variety**:
Switzerland boasts a wide range of mountain biking trails, from flowy forest tracks to tough alpine routes.
Explore singletrack tracks, forest walks, and gravel roads that wind through picturesque landscapes.
Choose trails that match your skill level and riding tastes, ranging from easy and family-friendly routes to technical and demanding descents.

**Swiss Bike Parks**:
Visit Swiss bike parks that cater especially to mountain bikers, offering a variety of trails, jumps, and features.
Bike parks like Verbier, Laax, and Lenzerheide provide lift-assisted access to downhill tracks and freeride routes.

Enjoy the thrill of riding berms, jumps, drops, and wooden features in a controlled and exhilarating setting.

**Enduro and All-Mountain Riding:**
Switzerland is famous for its epic enduro and all-mountain riding opportunities.
Discover trails that combine both climbing and technical descending, allowing you to explore the mountains while enjoying exciting downhill parts.
Areas like the Portes du Soleil region, Zermatt, and Engadin St. Moritz are famous for their extensive network of enduro paths.

**Alpine Adventures:**
Experience the thrill of alpine mountain riding by discovering high-altitude trails surrounded by stunning peaks.
Consider riding in areas like the Valais, Graubünden, or the Bernese Oberland, where you'll find trails that offer breathtaking views and challenging descents.
Keep in mind that alpine riding requires good fitness, technical skills, and suitable equipment.

**Bike Rental and Services:**
If you don't have your own mountain bike, rental shops are available in many Swiss towns and areas.
Ensure that the bike you rent is suitable for the area you'll be riding and properly fitted to your

measurements.

Take advantage of bike services, including repairs, maintenance, and gear storage, offered by local bike shops and hire companies.

**Trail Etiquette and Safety**:
Respect the paths, fellow riders, and the environment by following trail etiquette and practicing responsible riding.
Yield to hikers and other trail users, keep control of your bike, and ride within your limits.
Be prepared for changing weather conditions, carry important safety gear, and familiarize yourself with local trail regulations.

**Guided Tours and Bike Schools**:
Consider joining guided mountain bike tours or clinics run by experienced local riders or professional guides.
Guided trips offer the advantage of local knowledge, ensuring you experience the best trails and highlights of the area.
Bike schools provide coaching and skill-building lessons for riders of all levels, helping you improve technique and confidence.

**Trail Networks and Regions**:
Switzerland is home to numerous mountain biking regions and networks, each offering unique riding

experiences.

The Graubünden region, with places like Davos and Lenzerheide, boasts an extensive trail network, including flow trails, technical descents, and alpine adventures.

The Valais region, encompassing resorts such as Verbier and Zermatt, offers a mix of alpine terrain and bike parks, offering diverse riding options.

**Bike-Friendly Accommodations**:

Many Swiss facilities, including hotels, guesthouses, and mountain huts, cater to mountain bikers.

Look for bike-friendly places that provide secure bike storage, bike wash facilities, and local trail information.

Some accommodations also offer deals or guided tours specifically tailored to mountain bikers.

**Local Regulations and Environmental Awareness**:

Observe local laws and guidelines regarding trail usage and access.

Respect wildlife and natural habitats by sticking on designated trails and avoiding sensitive areas.

Contribute to trail maintenance and preservation efforts by participating in organized clean-up events or volunteering with local trail groups.

Switzerland's mountain biking trails offer an exciting and immersive way to explore its stunning landscapes. Whether you enjoy downhill thrills, cross-country adventures, or scenic alpine rides, Switzerland has it all. So hop on your mountain bike, find the beauty of the Swiss trails, and experience the excitement and freedom of mountain biking in this remarkable country.

Switzerland is a dream location for mountain biking enthusiasts, offering diverse landscapes, well-maintained trails, and breathtaking scenery. From thrilling downhill rides to scenic cross-country tracks, Switzerland has it all. Here are some of the best spots for mountain biking in Switzerland:

**Verbier**:
Located in the Swiss Alps, Verbier is known for its world-class mountain biking trails.
The bike park in Verbier features a range of downhill trails with different difficulty levels, jumps, and technical sections.
Enjoy breathtaking views of the nearby mountains as you navigate through the diverse terrain.

**Arosa-Lenzerheide**:
The Arosa-Lenzerheide region offers a network of trails perfect for all levels of riders.
Explore flow paths, downhill tracks, and cross-country routes surrounded by stunning alpine scenery.
The Bike Kingdom in Lenzerheide is a famous destination for mountain bikers, with well-marked trails

and dedicated facilities.

## Engadin St. Moritz:
Engadin St. Moritz is a mountain biking paradise, with a vast network of tracks that cater to all abilities.
Ride through picturesque valleys, alongside crystal-clear lakes, and across difficult alpine terrain.
The region hosts the prestigious Engadin Bike Giro, a yearly mountain biking event attracting riders from around the world.

## Flims-Laax:
The Flims-Laax region is known for its vast trail network and world-class bike park.
Enjoy flowy trails, technical descents, and freeride features in a beautiful alpine setting.
The Bike Arena in Flims-Laax hosts events like the Bike Kingdom Fest, drawing mountain biking enthusiasts from far and wide.

## Portes du Soleil:
The Portes du Soleil region straddles the border between Switzerland and France, giving an expansive mountain biking playground.
With over 600 kilometers (370 miles) of interconnected trails, it is one of the biggest mountain biking areas in the world.
Explore the varied terrain, including downhill runs,

cross-country tracks, and bike parks.

### Davos-Klosters:
Davos-Klosters is a mountain biking destination with trails suited for riders of all levels.
Ride through lush woods, open meadows, and challenging alpine terrain.
The Jakobshorn Bike Park in Davos offers a range of trails, jumps, and features for downhill and freeride fans.

### Crans-Montana:
Crans-Montana is a popular mountain biking destination, having a mix of natural and bike park trails.
Experience thrilling downhill rides, cross-country tracks, and panoramic views of the Rhône Valley.
The bike park in Crans-Montana includes jump lines, technical sections, and flowy trails.

### Interlaken:
The Interlaken area is not only famous for its stunning lakes but also offers exciting mountain biking opportunities.
Ride along beautiful trails that wind through the Swiss Alps, with views of the Eiger, Mönch, and Jungfrau peaks.
Explore the Grindelwald-First bike park, which offers steep tracks and freeride features.

**Jura Mountains**:

The Jura Mountains, located in the western part of Switzerland, offer a unique mountain biking adventure.

Ride through rolling hills, dense woods, and picturesque landscapes.

Discover a network of cross-country trails and enjoy the tranquility of this lesser-known mountain biking location.

When planning your mountain bike adventure in Switzerland, consider the time of year, trail conditions, and your skill level. It's important to ride responsibly, follow trail etiquette, and respect the environment. Switzerland's mountain biking destinations provide thrilling experiences and unforgettable scenery, making it a must-visit place for mountain biking enthusiasts.

## 7.4 Paragliding and Skydiving

Switzerland's stunning alpine landscapes and favorable weather conditions make it an ideal spot for adrenaline-pumping activities like paragliding and skydiving. Whether you want to soar through the skies with a paraglider or experience the exhilaration of skydiving, Switzerland offers excellent sites for these thrilling adventures. Here are some of the best places for paragliding and jumping in Switzerland:

**Interlaken**:

Interlaken, nestled between Lake Thun and Lake Brienz, is a famous hub for adventure sports, including paragliding and skydiving.

Experience the stunning views of the Swiss Alps as you take to the skies with a paraglider.

Tandem paragliding flights are offered, allowing you to fly with an experienced pilot and enjoy a safe and exhilarating experience.

For skydiving enthusiasts, Interlaken offers the chance to skydive from a plane, providing an adrenaline rush and a bird's-eye view of the area.

**Lauterbrunnen**:

Lauterbrunnen is a picturesque valley surrounded by majestic waterfalls and towering cliffs, offering a stunning setting for paragliding.

Take off from the cliffs and soar above the valley, having panoramic views of the lush green landscapes and snow-capped peaks.

Tandem paragliding trips in Lauterbrunnen allow you to experience the thrill of paragliding while accompanied by an expert pilot.

**Verbier**:

Verbier, located in the Valais region, offers excellent conditions for paragliding with its high-altitude location and stunning mountain views.

Soar above the famous Verbier ski resort and enjoy the

panoramic views of the nearby peaks.

Tandem paragliding flights are offered, allowing you to experience the sensation of flying while taking in the beauty of the Swiss Alps.

### Engelberg:

Engelberg, located in Central Switzerland, is a popular destination for both paragliding and skydiving.

Paragliders can launch from the slopes of Mount Titlis and glide through the alpine landscapes, marveling at the impressive peaks.

Skydiving enthusiasts can experience the thrill of freefalling from a plane, followed by a serene parachute descent with stunning views of the Engelberg area.

### Gstaad:

Gstaad is known for its luxurious ski resorts, but it also offers thrilling chances for paragliding.

Launch from the mountainside and soar above the idyllic landscapes of Gstaad, including rolling hills and picturesque towns.

Tandem paragliding flights in Gstaad allow you to enjoy the freedom of flying while admiring the beauty of the nearby area.

### Ticino:

Ticino, the Italian-speaking region of Switzerland, offers a unique backdrop for paragliding.

Launch from the steep cliffs of Monte Tamaro or Monte Generoso and glide above the scenic landscapes, including stunning lakes and charming towns.

Experience the thrill of flying in Ticino and enjoy the Mediterranean flair of the area.

**Skydiving Centers**:

In addition to paragliding, Switzerland is home to various skydiving centers that give tandem skydiving experiences.

Skydiving centers are spread throughout the country, including locations near Interlaken, Sion, and Emmen.

Skydiving allows you to experience the ultimate adrenaline rush as you jump from a plane and freefall through the sky, followed by a serene parachute landing.

Before participating in paragliding or skydiving activities, it's essential to ensure your safety by choosing reputable operators and experienced instructors. Confirm that they have proper certifications and adhere to safety rules. Also, consider the weather conditions and dress properly for your adventure.

Please note that paragliding and skydiving are weather-dependent activities, and it's important to check for any limits or limitations imposed by the local authorities or operators. Always prioritize your safety and follow the instructions given by the professionals.

Switzerland's breathtaking landscapes provide an

incredible setting for paragliding and skydiving, allowing you to experience the thrill of flight and take in the awe-inspiring beauty of the country from above. So, if you're wanting an unforgettable adventure, strap on your gear, take the leap, and enjoy the exhilaration of paragliding or skydiving in Switzerland.

## 7.5 Canyoning and Rafting

Switzerland's pristine rivers, gorges, and mountainous landscapes make it a perfect location for exhilarating water sports like canyoning and rafting. Whether you're wanting a thrilling adventure or simply want to immerse yourself in the beauty of nature, Switzerland offers excellent locations for canyoning and rafting experiences. Here are some of the best places for canyoning and rafting in Switzerland:

**Interlaken**:
Interlaken, situated between Lake Thun and Lake Brienz, is a famous hub for adventure sports, including canyoning and rafting.
Explore the stunning canyons and gorges of the area, rappelling down waterfalls, sliding down natural chutes, and jumping into crystal-clear pools.
The Lütschine River offers exciting rafting chances, with rapids ranging from mild to wild, perfect for both beginners and experienced rafters.

### Ticino:

Ticino, the Italian-speaking area of Switzerland, is known for its picturesque landscapes and beautiful rivers.

Discover the impressive canyons of the area, such as the Boggera Canyon and the Pontirone Canyon, where you can travel through narrow passages, slide down smooth rock slides, and jump into refreshing pools.

The Ticino River offers thrilling rafting experiences, with rapids that vary in intensity and breathtaking scenery along the way.

### Valais:

Valais, home to the majestic Swiss Alps, offers canyoning and rafting adventures surrounded by stunning mountain views.

Explore canyons like the Massa Gorge or the Trient Gorge, where you can rappel down cascading waterfalls, travel through tight slots, and swim in emerald pools.

The Rhône River in Valais offers thrilling rafting opportunities, with sections good for different skill levels and breathtaking views of the surrounding peaks.

### Engadin St. Moritz:

Engadin St. Moritz, located in the southeastern part of Switzerland, offers canyoning and rafting experiences in a beautiful mountain setting.

Descend canyons like the Swiss National Park Canyon or the Beverin Gorge, where you can abseil down waterfalls, slide down natural chutes, and discover the pristine natural surroundings.

The Inn River in Engadin St. Moritz offers exciting rafting options, with parts that range from calm floats to adrenaline-pumping rapids.

**Vaud**:

Vaud, a region located in western Switzerland, offers canyoning and rafting options amidst breathtaking landscapes.

Explore canyons like the Chauderon Canyon or the Pont du Diable Canyon, where you can travel through narrow gorges, jump into deep pools, and slide down natural slides.

The Simme River in Vaud provides exciting rafting experiences, with sections perfect for different skill levels and beautiful scenery along the way.

When participating in canyoning and rafting activities, always prioritize your safety by picking licensed and experienced guides or operators. They will provide the necessary equipment, guidance, and safety directions to ensure a thrilling yet safe experience. Additionally, follow the guidelines given by the professionals and respect the natural environment.

Canyoning and rafting in Switzerland offer unforgettable adventures, allowing you to connect with nature, feel the rush of adrenaline, and create lasting memories. So, gear up, accept the thrill, and enjoy the canyons and rivers of Switzerland through canyoning and rafting adventures.

## 7.6 Swiss Alpine Passes

Switzerland is famous for its beautiful alpine landscapes, and exploring the country's scenic mountain passes is a thrilling experience for outdoor enthusiasts. These alpine passes offer breathtaking views, difficult terrain, and a chance to immerse yourself in the beauty of the Swiss Alps. Here are some of the famous Swiss Alpine passes worth exploring:

**Grimsel Pass**:
Located in the Bernese Alps, the Grimsel Pass is a scenic mountain pass linking the cantons of Bern and Valais.
The pass offers stunning views of the nearby mountains, glacial lakes, and dramatic landscapes.
It's popular among cyclists and motorcyclists who seek the task of riding through its winding roads.

**Furka Pass**:
The Furka Pass is another spectacular alpine pass in the Swiss Alps, joining the cantons of Valais and Uri.
It's famous for its iconic winding road and the stunning

Rhône Glacier, which can be seen along the path.

The pass is a favorite among drivers, motorcyclists, and cyclists, offering a thrilling and scenic trip.

**Gotthard Pass**:

The Gotthard Pass is one of the most historic and notable mountain passes in Switzerland, connecting the cantons of Uri and Ticino.

It's known for its rich past, with remnants of the old cobblestone road and the historic Gotthard Hospice.

The pass offers breathtaking views of the Swiss Alps and is available by car, motorcycle, and bicycle.

**Susten Pass**:

The Susten Pass is a picturesque alpine pass located in the central Swiss Alps, linking the cantons of Bern and Uri.

It's famous for its stunning mountain vistas, hairpin bends, and the Susten Glacier.

The pass is a busy route for drivers, motorcyclists, and cyclists, giving a challenging and rewarding journey.

**Simplon Pass**:

The Simplon Pass links Switzerland with Italy, traversing the Pennine Alps between the cantons of Valais and Piedmont.

It's known for its technical marvels, including the Simplon Tunnel and the impressive stone arch bridge.

The pass offers panoramic views of the nearby mountains, making it a favorite among road trip enthusiasts.

## Klausen Pass:

The Klausen Pass is a scenic mountain pass located in central Switzerland, connecting the cantons of Uri and Glarus.

It's famous for its serpentine roads, dramatic scenery, and the charming Klausen Passhöhe village.

The pass is popular among motorcyclists and drivers wanting a challenging and rewarding alpine trip.

## Julier Pass:

The Julier Pass is an alpine pass found in the Graubünden region, connecting the Engadine Valley with the rest of Switzerland.

It gives stunning views of the Swiss Alps, picturesque valleys, and the sparkling Lake Silvaplana.

The pass is accessible by car, motorcycle, and bicycle, and it's a famous route for scenic drives.

These Swiss Alpine passes offer an incredible chance to experience the grandeur of the Swiss Alps, soak in breathtaking views, and embark on thrilling journeys through winding mountain roads. Whether you're driving, riding a motorbike, or cycling, these passes provide unforgettable adventures in the heart of Switzerland's alpine beauty.

## 7.7 Exploring Swiss Lakes

Switzerland is famous for its picturesque lakes, which offer serene beauty, crystal-clear waters, and a variety of recreational activities. Exploring the Swiss lakes is a delightful way to immerse yourself in nature, enjoy water sports, and experience the tranquility of the nearby scenery. Here are some of the famous Swiss lakes worth exploring:

**Lake Geneva (Lac Léman)**:
Lake Geneva is the largest lake in Switzerland, running across the French-Swiss border.
Explore the vibrant city of Geneva, located on the lake's southwestern side, known for its cultural attractions and historic landmarks.
Visit Lausanne, a charming lakeside city, home to the International Olympic Committee offices and the Olympic Museum.
Explore the medieval town of Montreux, famous for its annual jazz festival and the beautiful Château de Chillon.

**Lake Lucerne (Vierwaldstättersee):**
Lake Lucerne is one of Switzerland's most scenic lakes, encircled by majestic mountains and picturesque towns.
Take a boat trip on the lake to enjoy breathtaking views and visit iconic places like the Chapel Bridge in Lucerne.
Explore the city of Lucerne, known for its well-preserved old town, stunning waterfront

promenade, and vibrant culture scene.

Discover the lovely villages and towns along the shores of Lake Lucerne, such as Weggis, Vitznau, and Brunnen.

## Lake Zurich (Zürichsee):

Lake Zurich is a famous destination for both locals and tourists, located in the heart of the vibrant city of Zurich.

Take a leisurely walk along the lake promenade, enjoy a boat ride, or relax on one of the lakeside beaches.

Visit the picturesque towns of Rapperswil and Meilen, known for their charming old towns and historic sites.

Explore Zurich, Switzerland's largest city, with its bustling shopping streets, cultural attractions, and lively nightlife.

## Lake Thun (Thunersee):

Lake Thun is a stunning lake surrounded by the Bernese Alps, offering breathtaking views and a calm ambiance.

Take a scenic boat cruise on the lake to enjoy the mountain scenery and visit picturesque towns like Thun and Spiez.

Explore the medieval town of Thun, with its beautiful old town, famous castle, and charming lakeside promenade.

Engage in watersports activities like swimming, sailing, or paddleboarding in the clear waters of Lake Thun.

## Lake Brienz (Brienzersee):

Lake Brienz is another jewel among Swiss lakes, known for its turquoise-colored waters and dramatic mountain setting.

Take a boat trip on the lake to enjoy the stunning scenery and visit the charming town of Brienz.

Explore the Giessbach Falls, a majestic waterfall cascading into the lake, available by boat or hiking trail.

Engage in outdoor activities like kayaking, canoeing, or fishing in the peaceful surroundings of Lake Brienz.

**Lake Neuchâtel (Lac de Neuchâtel):**
Lake Neuchâtel is the largest lake entirely within Switzerland's borders, giving a serene and unspoiled setting.

Visit the city of Neuchâtel, located on the lake's northern side, known for its beautiful old town and the impressive Neuchâtel Castle.

Explore the charming wine-growing region of La Côte, located on the lake's southwestern shore, dotted with picturesque vineyards and wineries.

Enjoy water sports activities like sailing, windsurfing, or swimming in the clear waters of Lake Neuchâtel.

These Swiss lakes providea serene escape and a wealth of recreational possibilities. Whether you're seeking rest, water sports, or cultural exploration, these lakes offer something for everyone. Immerse yourself in the beauty of Switzerland's lakes, enjoy the surrounding landsapes, and make unforgettable memories in this picturesque country.

# Swiss Culture and Heritage

## 8.1 Swiss Cuisine and Traditional Dishes

Swiss cuisine is a reflection of the country's rich cultural heritage, with influences from nearby countries like Germany, France, and Italy. Swiss dishes are known for their hearty and comforting nature, often having cheese, chocolate, and regional ingredients. Here are some classic Swiss dishes that you must try during your visit:

**Fondue**:
Fondue is perhaps the most iconic Swiss dish, made of melted cheese served in a communal pot.
Dip pieces of bread into the bubbling cheese and enjoy the delicious combination of tastes.
Fondue versions include fondue Bourguignonne (meat fondue) and chocolate fondue for dessert.

**Raclette**:
Raclette is another famous cheese dish in Switzerland, made by melting a wheel of raclette cheese and scraping the melted part onto boiled potatoes, pickles, and onions.
It is a delicious and comforting dish that is perfect for sharing with friends and family.

**Rösti**:
Rösti is a Swiss-style grated potato pancake that is pan-fried until crispy on the outside and soft on the inside.
It is often served as a side dish and goes well with different toppings such as cheese, bacon, or fried eggs.

**Zürcher Geschnetzeltes**:
Zürcher Geschnetzeltes is a specialty from Zurich, having sliced veal cooked in a creamy mushroom sauce.

It is usually served with Rösti and is a favorite among locals and visitors alike.

**Swiss Chocolate**:

Switzerland is famous for its high-quality sweets, and indulging in Swiss chocolate is a must-do experience.

Visit local chocolatiers, explore chocolate factories, and taste a wide range of Swiss chocolate brands and flavors.

**Zopf**:

Zopf is a classic Swiss bread characterized by its braided shape and soft texture.

It is widely enjoyed for breakfast or as a side dish with butter and jam.

**Swiss Alps Honey**:

The Swiss Alps are home to varied flora and fauna, resulting in a variety of delicious honey flavors.

Try different types of Swiss Alps honey, each with its unique taste and aroma.

Aelplermagronen:

Aelplermagronen is a hearty Swiss pasta dish that blends macaroni with potatoes, cheese, and onions.

It is often served with applesauce and is a favorite comfort food in the Swiss Alps.

**Basel Läckerli**:

Basel Läckerli is a traditional Swiss gingerbread-like cookie from the city of Basel.

It is flavored with spices, honey, and candied fruits, making a delightful treat.

When dining in Switzerland, you'll also find a variety of foreign cuisines due to the country's multicultural influences. Additionally, don't forget to pair your meals with Swiss wines or try traditional Swiss beverages like Rivella (a famous Swiss soft drink) or a refreshing herbal infusion known as "Alpine herbal tea."

Exploring Swiss food is a delightful way to immerse yourself in the local culture and savor the unique flavors of the country. So indulge in Swiss culinary wonders, enjoy the comfort of traditional dishes, and treat your taste buds to the rich and diverse Swiss gastronomy.

## 8.2 Swiss Chocolate and Cheese

Switzerland is renowned globally for its exceptional chocolate and cheese. These two culinary delights are deeply rooted in Swiss culture and play a major role in the country's gastronomic heritage. Here's a better look at Swiss chocolate and cheese:

**Swiss Chocolate**:
Swiss chocolate is famous for its better quality, smooth texture, and rich flavor profiles.

Switzerland has a long history of chocolate making, dating back to the 19th century when pioneering chocolatiers revolutionized the business.

Swiss chocolate is crafted using high-quality cocoa beans, meticulous craftsmanship, and traditional methods.

The country boasts a wide range of chocolate types, from milk chocolate to dark chocolate, and an array of flavors and fillings.

Visit chocolate shops and factories to watch the chocolate-making process and indulge in tasting sessions to explore the diverse flavors.

**Swiss Cheese**:

Swiss cheese is renowned for its exceptional taste, quality, and iconic holey look.

Switzerland is home to a variety of cheese types, each originating from different regions and showcasing unique flavors and textures.

Emmental and Gruyère are two of the most famous Swiss cheeses, known for their nutty and creamy tastes.

Appenzeller, Tête de Moine, Raclette, and Vacherin Mont d'Or are other popular Swiss cheeses worth trying.

Visit cheese factories, alpine dairies, or local markets to watch the cheese-making process and learn about regional cheese specialties.

Pair Swiss cheese with fresh bread, dried meats, or fruits for a lovely tasting experience.

**Cheese Fondue and Raclette**:

Cheese fondue and raclette are traditional Swiss dishes that show the country's love for cheese.

Fondue involves dipping pieces of bread into a

communal pot of melted cheese, providing a convivial dining experience.

Raclette is the process of melting a wheel of cheese and putting the melted part onto accompaniments like potatoes, pickles, and onions.

Enjoying a fondue or raclette meal with friends and family is a cherished Swiss custom.

**Culinary Tourism**:

Switzerland offers numerous chances for chocolate and cheese enthusiasts to delve deeper into these gastronomic treasures.

Explore the Swiss Chocolate Chalet or Chocolate Train tours to learn about the chocolate-making process and delight in tastings.

Visit cheese museums, farms, or dairies to witness the cheese production and participate in cheese tastings.

Attend cheese festivals, such as the Montreux Cheese Festival, to celebrate and learn the diversity of Swiss cheese.

Swiss chocolate and cheese are not only delicious treats but also reflections of Swiss craftsmanship and culinary skill. When in Switzerland, take the time to enjoy the rich flavors of Swiss chocolate, indulge in a cheese fondue, and explore the diverse cheese types the country has to offer. It's a culinary journey that will leave a lasting impact on your taste buds and a deeper respect for Swiss culinary traditions.

## 8.3 Festivals and Events

Switzerland is known for its vibrant and diverse culture scene, with a wide array of festivals and events throughout the year. These celebrations highlight the country's traditions, heritage, music, art, sports, and more. Here are some of the famous festivals and events in Switzerland:

**Montreux Jazz Festival**:
Held in Montreux every July, the Montreux Jazz Festival is one of the world's most prestigious music events.
It includes renowned international artists and attracts music enthusiasts from around the world.
Enjoy a variety of jazz, blues, rock, and pop acts in the scenic setting of Lake Geneva.

**Basel Carnival (Basler Fasnacht):**
Basel Carnival is Switzerland's biggest carnival celebration, taking place in Basel during the three days running up to Ash Wednesday.
It is a bright and lively event featuring parades, music, elaborate costumes, and traditional masked characters.
Join the festivities, watch the Guggenmusik bands, and immerse yourself in the vibrant atmosphere.

**Locarno Film Festival**:
The Locarno Film Festival is a widely acclaimed film festival held annually in Locarno, in the Italian-speaking region of Switzerland.
It shows a diverse range of films, including both

mainstream and independent productions.

Experience open-air shows at the famous Piazza Grande and discover exceptional cinematic works.

### Lucerne Festival:

The Lucerne event is a world-renowned classical music event that takes place in Lucerne throughout the year.

It attracts acclaimed orchestras, conductors, and soloists, giving exceptional performances in different concert halls and outdoor venues.

Immerse yourself in the beauty of classical music and witness the talent of famous musicians.

### Fête de l'Escalade:

Celebrated in Geneva every December, the Fête de l'Escalade honors the city's defense against an attack in 1602.

The festival includes parades, historical reenactments, torchlight processions, and traditional costumes.

Participate in the festivities, try the traditional vegetable soup called "marmite," and enjoy the lively atmosphere.

### Zurich Street Parade:

The Zurich Street Parade is Europe's largest techno music festival, held yearly in Zurich.

It features electronic music, bright floats, and enthusiastic partygoers dancing through the streets.

Join the lively crowd, experience the pulsating beats, and revel in the vibrant energy of the event.

### Verbier Festival:

The Verbier Festival is a famous classical music festival

held in the mountain resort town of Verbier.

It draws together world-class musicians, young talents, and enthusiastic audiences.

Enjoy exceptional concerts and workshops in the beautiful alpine setting of Verbier.

**Lausanne Festival**:

The Lausanne event is a multidisciplinary arts event that takes place in Lausanne, showcasing a wide range of artistic expressions.

It includes theater performances, dance shows, visual arts exhibitions, music concerts, and more.

Immerse yourself in the cultural richness of Lausanne and experience the creativity of local and foreign artists.

These are just a few examples of the many holidays and events that grace the Swiss calendar throughout the year. Whether you're a music lover, art enthusiast, or simply wanting a lively atmosphere, Switzerland's festivals and events offer a diverse range of experiences that celebrate the country's culture and traditions. Make sure to check the event calendars and plan your visit properly to witness these vibrant celebrations firsthand.

## 8.4 Traditional Swiss Music and Folklore

Switzerland has a rich heritage of traditional music and folklore that represents the country's diverse cultural influences and regional traditions. Exploring Swiss music and folklore offers a unique glimpse into the history, customs, and traditions of the Swiss people. Here are some key features of traditional Swiss music and folklore:

**Yodeling**:

Yodeling is a unique vocal technique that involves alternating between chest and head voice, creating a melodic and rhythmic sound.

It is an iconic element of Swiss music and is often played in the alpine regions of Switzerland.

Experience the melodic tunes and unique vocal stylings of yodeling at traditional Swiss music events or mountain festivals.

**Alphorn**:

The alphorn is a traditional Swiss musical instrument made of wood, usually measuring several meters in length.

It produces deep, resonant tones and is often played in alpine areas and during traditional Swiss festivals.

Witness the powerful sounds of the alphorn during performances or even try playing one yourself under expert direction.

**Schwyzerörgeli:**

The schwyzerörgeli is a type of accordion usually associated with Swiss folk music.

It is characterized by its distinctive sound and is often played during traditional dances and festive events.

Listen to the lively melodies of the schwyzerörgeli at folk music festivals or traditional Swiss music shows.

**Fasnacht**:

Fasnacht is a traditional Swiss carnival celebration that takes place in different regions across the country.

It features colorful costumes, masks, parades, and traditional music acts.

Experience the vibrant atmosphere of Fasnacht and watch the traditional music and dances associated with this festive event.

**Swiss Folk Dances**:

Swiss folk dances are an important part of the country's cultural heritage.

Each area has its own unique dances, costumes, and music styles, showcasing the diversity of Swiss folklore.

Attend folk dance performances or even join in dance workshops to learn traditional Swiss dance moves.

**Appenzell Music**:

The Appenzell area in Switzerland is known for its lively traditional music, characterized by accordion melodies and lively rhythms.

Experience the lively and energetic sounds of Appenzell music during local festivals or traditional music events.

**Flag Throwing:**

Flag throwing is a traditional Swiss performance art that includes acrobatics, dance, and the skillful manipulation of large flags.

It is often followed by traditional music and is a sight to behold during festivals and cultural events.

Exploring traditional Swiss music and folklore offers a

unique chance to immerse yourself in the rich cultural heritage of the country. Attend traditional music performances, witness folk dances, listen to the melodic tunes of yodeling and alphorn, and experience the lively spirit of Swiss culture. These cultural expressions provide a deeper understanding of Switzerland's traditions and add to a memorable and immersive travel experience.

## 8.5 Swiss Watches and Clocks

Switzerland is famous worldwide for its precision craftsmanship and mastery in watchmaking. Swiss watches and clocks are synonymous with great quality, precision, and timeless elegance. Here's a closer look at the importance of Swiss watches and clocks:

**Swiss Watchmaking Tradition**:
Switzerland has a long-standing tradition of watchmaking that goes back several centuries.
Swiss watchmakers are known for their meticulous attention to detail, precision engineering, and commitment to craftsmanship.
The country's watchmaking industry has set the worldwide standard for excellence, making Swiss watches highly sought after by watch enthusiasts and collectors.

**Swiss Watch Brands**:

Switzerland is home to some of the world's most prestigious watch brands, known for their quality, innovation, and iconic designs.

Brands like Rolex, Patek Philippe, Omega, TAG Heuer, and many others have received international acclaim for their exceptional timepieces.

Swiss watch brands offer a wide range of styles, from classic and elegant to sporty and avant-garde, responding to different tastes and preferences.

**Watchmaking Centers**:

Switzerland has several watchmaking centers that are synonymous with success in the industry.

Geneva, known as the "Capital of Haute Horlogerie," is home to famous luxury watch brands and hosts the annual Salon International de la Haute Horlogerie (SIHH) watch fair.

The watchmaking region of Neuchâtel is another notable area, housing many prestigious watch manufacturers and institutions.

Other notable watchmaking centers include La Chaux-de-Fonds and Le Locle, both recognized as UNESCO World Heritage Sites for their horological importance.

**Swiss Clocks**:

In addition to watches, Switzerland is also famous for its

precision-crafted clocks.

The country's clockmaking heritage spans centuries and has contributed to the development of various types of clocks, including mechanical, pendulum, and cuckoo clocks.

Swiss clocks are prized for their accuracy, intricate designs, and exceptional workmanship.

**Clock Towers**:

Switzerland is adorned with numerous iconic clock towers, which not only serve as timekeeping devices but also symbolize the country's architectural and cultural history.

The Zytglogge clock tower in Bern, the Clock Tower of the St. Pierre Cathedral in Geneva, and the Clock Tower in Lausanne are just a few examples of the amazing clock towers found throughout Switzerland.

**Horological Museums**:

Switzerland boasts several horological museums committed to preserving the history and artistry of watchmaking and clockmaking.

The Patek Philippe Museum in Geneva, the Omega Museum in Biel/Bienne, and the International Watchmaking Museum in La Chaux-de-Fonds offer insights into the evolution of timekeeping tools and the craftsmanship behind Swiss watches and clocks.

Swiss watches and clocks reflect a harmonious blend of tradition, innovation, and precision. They not only serve as practical timekeeping devices but also as exquisite works of art and symbols of Swiss craftsmanship. When in Switzerland, explore watchmaking centers, visit horological museums, and enjoy the mastery of Swiss watches and clocks. It's a chance to appreciate the timeless beauty and engineering excellence that have made Switzerland a global leader in the industry.

## 8.6 Museums and Art Galleries

Switzerland is home to a wealth of museums and art galleries, showing a diverse range of artistic and cultural treasures. From historical artifacts and modern art to scientific discoveries and interactive exhibitions, Switzerland offers a rich cultural landscape for museum enthusiasts. Here are some famous museums and art galleries worth exploring:

**Kunsthaus Zurich:**
Located in Zurich, the Kunsthaus is one of Switzerland's most famous art museums.
It holds an extensive collection of European art, with works ranging from the Middle Ages to the present day.
Explore masterpieces by famous artists such as Monet, Van Gogh, Picasso, and Chagall.

**Swiss National Museum**:

Situated in Zurich, the Swiss National Museum is dedicated to Swiss cultural history.

Discover artifacts, exhibits, and interactive displays that illustrate the country's history, including art, design, and traditional crafts.

The museum building itself is an architectural gem, showing a blend of Gothic and Renaissance styles.

**The Olympic Museum**:

Located in Lausanne, the Olympic Museum is a must-visit for sports fans and Olympic history buffs.

Learn about the past of the Olympic Games through interactive exhibits, multimedia presentations, and a vast collection of Olympic memorabilia.

Enjoy panoramic views of Lake Geneva and discover the beautiful park surrounding the museum.

**Beyeler Foundation**:

Situated in Riehen near Basel, the Beyeler Foundation is a famous art museum set within a stunning architectural masterpiece.

It holds a remarkable collection of modern and contemporary art, including works by renowned artists like Picasso, Monet, and Warhol.

The museum is surrounded by beautiful gardens, giving a tranquil setting to appreciate art.

**Fondation Pierre Gianadda**:

Located in Martigny, the Fondation Pierre Gianadda is a culture complex that hosts a variety of exhibitions throughout the year.

Explore its art museum, which showcases works by renowned artists, as well as its automobile museum, showing a remarkable collection of vintage cars.

The foundation is set against the backdrop of the majestic Swiss Alps, offering a picturesque setting.

**Museum Tinguely**:

Situated in Basel, the Museum Tinguely is dedicated to the works of Swiss artist Jean Tinguely.

Discover Tinguely's unique kinetic art sculptures, which are defined by movement and playfulness.

The museum also hosts temporary exhibitions showing contemporary artists.

**The Museum of Art and History Geneva**:

Located in Geneva, the Museum of Art and History houses a huge collection of art, archaeology, and applied arts.

Explore its extensive collection of paintings, sculptures, and decorative arts, as well as archaeological artifacts from different cultures.

The museum's diverse exhibitions offer a thorough overview of art and history.

**Swiss Museum of Transport**:

Situated in Lucerne, the Swiss Museum of Transport is a fascinating museum dedicated to all types of transportation.

Discover the history of trains, planes, cars, and more through interactive exhibits, simulators, and historical artifacts.

The museum also houses a planetarium and an IMAX theater.

These are just a few examples of the many museums and art spaces in Switzerland. Whether you're interested in art, history, science, or technology, there's a museum or library to cater to your interests. Immerse yourself in Switzerland's cultural offerings, admire remarkable artworks, and delve into the country's interesting past through its museums and art galleries.

## 8.7 UNESCO World Heritage Sites in Switzerland

Switzerland boasts a remarkable array of UNESCO World Heritage Sites that highlight its natural beauty, architectural excellence, and cultural importance. These places are recognized for their outstanding universal value and contribute to the preservation of humanity's cultural and natural heritage. Here are some UNESCO World Heritage Sites in Switzerland:

**Swiss Alps Jungfrau-Aletsch**:

This site includes the Jungfrau-Aletsch-Bietschhorn region, located in the Swiss Alps.

It offers breathtaking mountain landscapes, including the Aletsch Glacier, the largest glacier in the Alps.

Explore the alpine ecosystems, stunning peaks, and picturesque valleys, which are home to diverse flora and wildlife.

**Lavaux Vineyards**:

The Lavaux Vineyards are located along the shores of Lake Geneva in the Vaud region.

This terraced wine-growing area stretches over 30 kilometers and is renowned for its scenic beauty and traditional vineyard practices.

Take a walk through the vineyards, taste local wines, and enjoy panoramic views of Lake Geneva.

**Convent of St. Gall**:

Located in the town of St. Gallen, the Convent of St. Gall is a medieval abbey complex that goes back to the 8th century.

It includes the Abbey Library, which houses a vast collection of medieval manuscripts, and the Abbey Church, known for its impressive baroque building.

Explore the rich history and cultural heritage of this UNESCO-listed place.

**Old City of Bern**:
The Old City of Bern, Switzerland's capital, is a well-preserved medieval city.
It is known for its artistic integrity, with numerous medieval buildings, narrow streets, and arcades.
Discover Bern's famous sites, including the Clock Tower (Zytglogge), Bern Cathedral, and the Federal Palace.

**Monte San Giorgio:**
Monte San Giorgio is a mountain found on the Swiss-Italian border.
It is recognized for its exceptional fossil record, which offers valuable insights into marine life during the Triassic period.
Visit the fossil museum and discover the mountain's geological wonders.

**Abbey of St. John at Müstair**:
Situated in the canton of Graubünden, the Abbey of St. John at Müstair is a Carolingian monastery built in the 8th century.
It features well-preserved frescoes going back to the 9th century, depicting religious scenes and providing a glimpse into medieval art.
Explore the abbey complex, including the church and the museum, to appreciate its historical and artistic importance.
Rhaetian Railway in the Albula/Bernina Landscapes:

This UNESCO World Heritage Site includes the Albula and Bernina railway lines, which cross the stunning landscapes of the Swiss Alps.

Experience a scenic train trip through breathtaking mountain scenery, dramatic viaducts, and tunnels that exemplify remarkable engineering feats.

These are just a few examples of the UNESCO World Heritage Sites in Switzerland. Each site showcases a unique aspect of the country's natural and cultural heritage, giving visitors a chance to explore and enjoy Switzerland's outstanding universal value.

# Accommodation Options

## 9.1 Hotels and Resorts

Switzerland offers a wide range of accommodation options to fit different preferences and budgets. Whether you're looking for luxury hotels, cozy mountain lodges, or budget-friendly lodging, there are plenty of choices available. Here are some famous hotels and resorts in Switzerland:

**The Dolder Grand (Zurich):**

A luxurious 5-star hotel located in Zurich, giving panoramic views of the city and Lake Zurich.

The hotel features elegant rooms, a spa, several fine dining places, and impeccable service.

**Badrutt's Palace Hotel (St. Moritz):**

A legendary luxury hotel located in the heart of St. Moritz, renowned for its glamorous atmosphere and alpine charm.

It offers opulent rooms, world-class dining choices, a lavish spa, and access to exclusive winter sports activities.

**Baur au Lac (Zurich):**

A prestigious 5-star hotel located in Zurich, facing Lake Zurich and the Alps.

The hotel mixes elegance and sophistication with top-notch service, luxurious rooms, and exquisite dining experiences.

**Kulm Hotel (St. Moritz):**

An iconic hotel in St. Moritz, giving a blend of traditional charm and modern comforts.

The hotel boasts well-appointed rooms, gourmet restaurants, a luxury spa, and breathtaking views of the Engadin mountains.

**The Chedi Andermatt (Andermatt):**

A stunning 5-star hotel nestled in the Swiss Alps in Andermatt, giving a seamless blend of modern design and alpine chic.

It features luxurious rooms, multiple dining choices, a spacious spa, and direct access to world-class skiing.

**La Réserve Genève Hotel, Spa and Villas (Geneva):**

A luxury hotel located on the shores of Lake Geneva, giving elegant rooms, exceptional service, and a tranquil spa.

The hotel also provides private villas with beautiful lake views for a more exclusive and intimate experience.

**The Chedi Zermatt (Zermatt):**

A luxurious mountain resort located in Zermatt, offering magnificent views of the Matterhorn and exceptional amenities.

It boasts beautifully designed rooms, gourmet dining choices, an extensive spa, and a ski-in/ski-out location.

**Victoria-Jungfrau Grand Hotel & Spa (Interlaken):**

A historic 5-star hotel located in Interlaken, blending old-world charm with modern elegance.

It offers spacious rooms, multiple restaurants, a luxury spa, and easy access to the Jungfrau region's natural wonders.

**Gstaad Palace (Gstaad):**

A renowned luxury hotel nestled in the Swiss Alps in Gstaad, offering majestic views, opulent accommodations, and world-class services.

It features luxurious rooms, fine dining choices, a lavish spa, and a wide range of recreational activities.

**Hotel Schweizerhof Luzern (Lucerne):**

A stylish hotel located in the heart of Lucerne, known for its elegant rooms, excellent service, and breathtaking views of Lake Lucerne.

It offers a range of dining choices, a rooftop spa, and easy access to Lucerne's attractions.

These are just a few examples of the exceptional hotels and resorts offered in Switzerland. Depending on your preferred location and budget, you can explore different choices that suit your needs. It's advisable to book in advance, especially during peak travel seasons, to secure your desired lodgings and make the most of your stay in Switzerland.

## 9.2 Guesthouses and Bed & Breakfasts

If you prefer a more intimate and cozy accommodation experience, Switzerland offers a range of guesthouses and bed & breakfasts that provide personalized service and a warm, homely environment. Here are some famous guesthouses and bed & breakfasts in Switzerland:

**Chalet Martin (Zermatt):**
A charming guesthouse located in Zermatt, giving comfortable rooms with stunning views of the nearby mountains.
The guesthouse offers a cozy ambiance, wonderful breakfast, and a friendly, welcoming atmosphere.

**Gästehaus Casa Collina (Lucerne):**
A family-run bed & breakfast situated in Lucerne, offering cozy rooms and a tranquil setting overlooking Lake Lucerne.
Guests can enjoy a delicious breakfast, personalized service, and a peaceful garden to rest in.

**Hotel Garni Bären (Interlaken):**
A well-established bed & breakfast set in the heart of Interlaken, offering comfortable rooms and a hearty Swiss breakfast.
The friendly hosts provide local tips and assistance to ensure a pleasant stay in the beautiful Bernese Oberland

area.

### BnB Chalet la Colline (Gruyères):

A charming bed & breakfast set in the picturesque town of Gruyères, known for its famous cheese.

The cozy rooms, warm welcome, and panoramic views of the Swiss countryside make for a delightful stay.

### Berggasthaus Aescher-Wildkirchli (Appenzell):

An iconic mountain guesthouse situated in the Alpstein region of Appenzell.

It offers rustic accommodations with breathtaking views, traditional Swiss food, and easy access to hiking trails.

### Bed and Breakfast Gantrisch Cottage (Gantrisch Nature Park):

A lovely bed & breakfast located in the tranquil Gantrisch Nature Park, near Bern.

The cozy rooms, homemade breakfast, and serene surroundings make it an ideal getaway for nature lovers.

### Gästehaus Sonnenhalde (Zurich):

A family-run guesthouse located in a peaceful residential area of Zurich, offering comfortable rooms and a hearty breakfast.

The friendly hosts offer personalized service and helpful tips for exploring the city.

### B&B Haus zur Trülle (Basel):

A charming bed & breakfast located in the historic old town of Basel.

It offers cozy rooms with a mix of modern comfort and traditional Swiss charm, along with a delicious breakfast.

**Pension St. Jakob (Engelberg):**

A welcoming guesthouse set in the mountain village of Engelberg, offering comfortable rooms and a generous breakfast.

The hosts provide a warm atmosphere and important insights for exploring the surrounding Swiss Alps.

**BnB Chalet Gafri (Saas-Fee):**

A cozy bed & breakfast nestled in the car-free town of Saas-Fee, surrounded by stunning alpine scenery.

It gives comfortable rooms, a homemade breakfast, and a peaceful setting.

These guesthouses and bed & breakfasts provide an authentic Swiss experience, with personalized service, local charm, and warm welcome. They are ideal for travelers wanting a more intimate and homey accommodation option while exploring the beauty of Switzerland. Remember to check availability and make plans in advance, especially during peak travel seasons, to secure your desired stay.

## 9.3 Vacation Rentals and Apartments

For travelers seeking a home-away-from-home experience, vacation rentals and apartments in Switzerland offer the flexibility and comfort of having your own room. They are particularly ideal for families, groups, or those looking for a longer stay. Here are some reputable vacation rentals and apartment choices in Switzerland:

**Airbnb (www.airbnb.com):**

Airbnb offers a wide range of vacation rentals and apartments throughout Switzerland, allowing you to choose from various places, sizes, and amenities.

From cozy apartments in city centers to spacious chalets in the mountains, Airbnb offers options to fit different preferences and budgets.

**HomeAway (www.homeaway.com):**

HomeAway features a range of vacation rentals and apartments in Switzerland, ranging from city apartments to countryside cottages.

You can browse through the listings, filter based on your requirements, and speak directly with the property owners.

**Interhome (www.interhome.com):**

Interhome is a leading vacation rental service that offers a range of apartments, chalets, and holiday homes in Switzerland.

They have properties in popular destinations such as Zermatt, Verbier, Interlaken, and more, offering options for every type of traveler.

**Booking.com (www.booking.com):**

Booking.com offers a wide range of accommodation choices, including vacation rentals and apartments, in Switzerland.

You can search for apartments based on your chosen

location, amenities, and guest reviews, making it easier to find the right fit.

**Switzerland Tourism (www.myswitzerland.com):**

The official website of Switzerland Tourism offers a section dedicated to vacation rentals and apartments.

You can look for available properties, view photos, and book directly through the website.

**Engadin Apartments (www.engadinapartments.ch):**

Engadin Apartments specializes in holiday rentals in the Engadine region, offering a variety of apartments and chalets in famous destinations like St. Moritz, Pontresina, and Sils-Maria.

**Wengen Apartments (www.wengenapartments.com):**

Wengen Apartments gives a selection of self-catering apartments in the charming alpine village of Wengen, located in the Jungfrau region.

The apartments offer beautiful mountain views and easy access to hiking and skiing sports.

**Zermatt Chalets & Apartments (www.zermattapartmentrentals.com):**

Zermatt Chalets & Apartments specializes in holiday rentals in Zermatt, offering a range of apartments and chalets in this famous Swiss mountain resort.

The properties provide a comfortable and convenient base for experiencing the breathtaking Matterhorn area.

When booking vacation rentals or apartments, consider factors such as location, features, and reviews to ensure a satisfying stay. Make sure to interact with the property owners or agencies to clarify any questions and secure your booking in advance, especially during peak travel periods.

## 9.4 Camping and Caravan Sites

For travelers who love the great outdoors and prefer a more adventurous accommodation choice, Switzerland offers a range of camping and caravan sites. These sites provide a chance to immerse yourself in nature, enjoy scenic landscapes, and have access to different outdoor activities. Here are some famous camping and caravan sites in Switzerland:

**Camping Jungfrau (Lauterbrunnen):**

Located in the picturesque Lauterbrunnen Valley, Camping Jungfrau is a well-equipped campground with amazing mountain views.

It offers tent pitches, caravan sites, and rental accommodations, along with features such as modern sanitary facilities, restaurants, and outdoor sports facilities.

**Camping Manor Farm (Interlaken)**:

Situated near Interlaken, Camping Manor Farm is a family-friendly campsite set between Lake Thun and Lake Brienz.

It offers spacious camping pitches, caravan sites, and rental accommodations, with facilities including a swimming pool, playground, and on-site restaurant.

**Camping TCS Disentis (Disentis):**

Located in the beautiful Disentis area, Camping TCS Disentis offers a tranquil setting surrounded by mountains and rivers.

The campground offers camping pitches and caravan sites, along with amenities such as a restaurant, playground, and direct access to hiking and biking trails.

**Camping du Botza (Valais):**

Situated in the Valais region near the town of Sion, Camping du Botza is a peaceful campsite with sweeping mountain views.

It offers camping pitches, caravan sites, and rental accommodations, with features including a swimming pool, restaurant, and outdoor sports areas.

**Camping Vitznau (Vitznau):**

Located on the shores of Lake Lucerne, Camping Vitznau offers a beautiful lakeside camping experience.

The campsite offers camping pitches and caravan sites, with direct access to the lake for swimming and water sports activities.

**Camping Manor Farm (Zurich):**

Situated on the outskirts of Zurich, Camping Manor Farm offers a convenient base for experiencing the city and its surrounding areas.

It offers camping pitches, caravan sites, and rental accommodations, along with amenities like a swimming pool, playground, and on-site restaurant.

**Camping Gamp (Grindelwald):**

Nestled in the charming town of Grindelwald, Camping Gamp offers breathtaking views of the surrounding mountains.

The campsite offers camping pitches, caravan sites, and rental accommodations, with services including a restaurant, playground, and direct access to hiking trails.

**Camping Seefeld (Zurich):**

Located on the shores of Lake Zurich, Camping Seefeld offers a peaceful lakeside camping experience within close access to Zurich.

It offers camping pitches, caravan sites, and rental accommodations, with amenities like a swimming pool, restaurant, and water sports equipment rental.

When camping or staying in a caravan, it's important to check the campsite's facilities, reservation policies, and any specific laws or requirements. Some campsites may have limited availability, especially during peak seasons, so it's wise to make reservations in advance. Additionally, be sure to follow responsible camping practices and respect the environment while loving your outdoor adventure in Switzerland.

## 9.5 Mid-Range Accommodation

If you're looking for comfortable and reasonably priced accommodation choices in Switzerland, there are several mid-range hotels that offer a balance between quality and affordability. These hotels provide modern amenities, handy locations, and a pleasant stay without breaking the bank. Here are some recommended mid-range accommodation choices in Switzerland:

**Hotel Allegra (Zurich):**

A stylish hotel located near Zurich Airport, having spacious rooms, a fitness center, and a complimentary airport shuttle.

It offers easy access to the city center and is suitable for both business and leisure travelers.

**Hotel Montana Zürich (Zurich):**

Situated in the heart of Zurich, Hotel Montana offers comfortable rooms with modern amenities and a free breakfast buffet.

It is conveniently situated near major attractions, shopping areas, and public transportation.

**Hotel Krebs (Interlaken):**

Located in the center of Interlaken, Hotel Krebs offers cozy rooms, a restaurant serving Swiss and foreign cuisine, and a rooftop terrace with panoramic views.

It is within walking distance of the Interlaken Ost train station and offers easy access to outdoor activities in the Jungfrau area.

**Hotel Touring (Lucerne):**

A well-appointed hotel located near Lucerne's train station and within walking distance of the Old Town.

Hotel Touring offers comfortable rooms, a bar, and a

breakfast buffet, making it a convenient base for experiencing Lucerne's attractions.

**Hotel ibis Styles Basel City (Basel):**

Located in the center of Basel, this hotel features stylish and modern rooms, a complimentary breakfast, and a fitness center.

It is within walking distance of the Old Town, Basel's key attractions, and public transportation.

**Hotel Crystal (Zermatt):**

Situated in Zermatt, Hotel Crystal offers comfortable rooms, a wellness area with a sauna and steam room, and a restaurant serving Swiss and international food.

The hotel is conveniently located near the train station and offers easy access to hiking and skiing activities.

**Hotel ibis Lausanne Centre (Lausanne):**

A modern hotel located in the heart of Lausanne, having comfortable rooms, a bar, and a 24-hour snack service.

It is within walking distance of the Lausanne train station, the Olympic Museum, and the city's sights.

**Hotel Bella Vista (Locarno):**

Situated in Locarno, Hotel Bella Vista offers cozy rooms, a garden deck with panoramic views of Lake Maggiore, and a complimentary breakfast buffet.

The hotel is a short walk away from the lake promenade and offers easy access to the region's natural beauty.

**Hotel Astoria (Geneva):**

Located in the center of Geneva, Hotel Astoria offers comfortable rooms, a breakfast buffet, and a handy location near Lake Geneva and the city's main attractions.

It is within walking distance of the train station and offers easy access to public transportation.

**Hotel Alpenblick (Bern)**:

A family-run hotel located in a quiet residential area of Bern, offering comfortable rooms, a garden terrace, and a complimentary breakfast buffet.

The hotel is a short tram ride away from Bern's city center and its famous sights.

These mid-range hotels provide a comfortable and convenient stay while giving good value for your money. It's advisable to check availability and make reservations in advance, especially during peak travel seasons, to secure your preferred accommodation.

## 9.6 Hostels

For budget-conscious travelers or those looking to meet fellow travelers, hostels in Switzerland offer affordable accommodation choices with a social and friendly atmosphere. These hostels provide sharing dormitory rooms or private rooms at reasonable prices. Here are some suggested hostels in Switzerland:

**City Backpacker - Hotel Biber (Zurich)**:

Located in the heart of Zurich's old town, this hostel offers dormitory rooms with comfortable beds and a common kitchen.

It has a lively common area, where guests can socialize and meet fellow tourists.

**Balmer's Hostel (Interlaken):**

Situated in Interlaken, Balmer's Hostel offers a range of accommodation options, including dormitory rooms, private rooms, and Swiss-style chalets.

The hostel features an outdoor bar, a large garden, and different activities for guests, such as live music and BBQ nights.

**Backpackers Villa Sonnenhof (Interlaken):**

A popular hostel in Interlaken, giving dormitory rooms, private rooms, and self-catering apartments.

The hostel offers a spacious common area, a well-equipped kitchen, and a cozy lounge with a fireplace.

**Youth Hostel Lucerne:**

Located near Lake Lucerne, the Youth Hostel in Lucerne offers cozy dormitory rooms and private rooms.

It features a terrace with panoramic views, a game room, and a restaurant serving Swiss food.

**Geneva Hostel:**

Situated near Lake Geneva, the Geneva Hostel offers dormitory rooms and individual rooms.

The hostel provides a shared kitchen, a bar, and a garden terrace, and it offers a free Geneva Transport Card to guests.

**Zermatt Youth Hostel:**

A cozy hostel in Zermatt, offering dormitory rooms and

private rooms with amazing views of the Matterhorn.

The hostel has a shared kitchen, a cozy lounge, and a terrace, and it provides easy access to hiking and skiing activities.

**Luzern Youth Hostel**:

Located in Lucerne, Luzern Youth Hostel offers shared rooms and private rooms.

The hostel features a garden deck, a common room with board games, and a bar serving drinks and snacks.

**Basel BackPack**:

Situated in Basel's old town, Basel BackPack offers communal rooms and private rooms.

The hostel offers a shared kitchen, a lounge area, and a garden terrace, and it is within walking distance of Basel's main attractions.

**Interlaken Youth Hostel**:

A modern hostel in Interlaken, giving dormitory rooms and private rooms.

The hostel features a big outdoor area, a bar, and a restaurant, and it offers various outdoor activities and excursions.

**St. Moritz Youth Hostel**:

Located in St. Moritz, this hostel offers shared rooms and private rooms with mountain views.

The hostel provides a common room, a games area, and a self-catering kitchen, and it offers cheap ski passes during winter.

These hostels offer affordable accommodation choices with communal places that encourage interaction among travelers. They are an excellent choice for budget travelers or those wanting a vibrant and social atmosphere during their stay in Switzerland. Be sure to check availability and make plans in advance, especially during peak travel seasons.

# Dining and Culinary Experiences

## 10.1 Restaurants and Cafés

Switzerland is known for its diverse culinary scene, having a range of restaurants and cafés that cater to various tastes and preferences. Whether you're seeking traditional Swiss cuisine, foreign dishes, or trendy café culture, Switzerland has it all. Here are some types of places and cafés you can explore:

**Traditional Swiss Restaurants**:
These restaurants showcase genuine Swiss cuisine, featuring dishes such as fondue, raclette, rösti (Swiss-style grated and fried potatoes), and traditional Alpine specialties.
Look for cozy chalet-style restaurants or rustic mountain restaurants to experience the traditional Swiss dining scene.

**International Cuisine Restaurants:**
Switzerland's multiculturalism is reflected in its diverse international dining choices. You can find restaurants offering Italian, French, Asian, Mediterranean, and other international cuisines.
Explore neighborhoods with lively dining scenes, such as Zurich's Niederdorf area, Geneva's Paquis district, or Basel's St. Johann neighborhood.

**Gourmet and Michelin-Starred Restaurants**:

Switzerland is home to several famous gourmet and Michelin-starred restaurants that offer exceptional dining experiences.

These places focus on creative and refined cuisine, often highlighting local and seasonal ingredients. They provide a chance to indulge in culinary excellence.

Farm-to-Table and Locally Sourced Restaurants:

Switzerland's agricultural heritage is showcased in farm-to-table restaurants that value locally sourced ingredients.

These establishments highlight regional produce, cheeses, meats, and wines, giving a true taste of Swiss terroir and sustainability.

**Lakeside and Waterfront Dining**:

Many Swiss cities and towns are located near lakes, offering the chance to dine with beautiful waterfront views.

Look for restaurants and cafés along the shores of Lake Geneva, Lake Zurich, Lake Lucerne, or Lake Thun to enjoy scenic views while dining.

**Trendy Cafés and Bakeries**:

Switzerland has a lively café culture, with numerous trendy cafés and bakeries serving freshly brewed coffee, pastries, sandwiches, and light meals.

Explore charming streets in cities like Zurich, Geneva, or Bern to find cozy cafés with a relaxed ambiance and delicious treats.

**Street Food and Food Markets**:

Switzerland's cities often have vibrant food markets and street food scenes, offering a range of tasty and affordable options.

Visit markets like Zurich's Im Viadukt, Geneva's Carouge Market, or Bern's Bundesplatz Market to savor local snacks, artisanal goods, and street food delicacies.

**Alpine Huts and Mountain Restaurants**:
When visiting the Swiss Alps, you'll come across charming alpine huts and mountain restaurants offering hearty meals and stunning views.

These places provide a unique dining experience in the middle of picturesque landscapes, making them ideal for hikers, skiers, and nature lovers.

When dining out, it's advisable to make reservations, especially for gourmet places or popular establishments, as they can get busy. Additionally, familiarize yourself with Swiss eating customs, such as tipping etiquette and restaurant opening hours, to ensure a smooth dining experience.

Here is a list of recommended cafes and restaurants in Switzerland that offer a range of culinary experiences:

Restaurants in Zurich:

**Kronenhalle**: A legendary restaurant offering classic Swiss dishes in an elegant setting.

**Restaurant Didi's Frieden**: Known for its classic Swiss cuisine, including fondue and raclette.

**Zeughauskeller**: Offers hearty Swiss favorites, such as sausages, roasts, and rösti.

**Restaurant Swiss Chuchi**: A charming restaurant offering authentic Swiss dishes, including cheese fondue and Alpine classics.

**Restaurant Blindekuh**: Experience dining in total darkness while enjoying a surprise menu of seasonal dishes.

Restaurants in Geneva:

**Café du Centre**: A popular spot for classic Swiss cuisine, including cheese fondue and raclette.

**Auberge de Saviese**: Specializes in Swiss Valais cuisine, serving dishes like raclette, cured meats, and fondue.

**Café des Négociants**: Known for its seasonal Swiss and French cuisine, with a focus on fresh and local products.

**Chez Ma Cousine**: Famous for its roasted chicken and simple yet delicious Swiss meals.

**Cottage Café**: A cozy café serving a range of Swiss and international dishes, as well as homemade pastries and cakes.

Restaurants in Lucerne:

**Old Swiss House**: Offers a refined dining experience with a focus on traditional Swiss food.

Wirtshaus Taube: Known for its rustic ambiance and classic Swiss dishes like fondue, raclette, and schnitzel.

Restaurant Balances: Offers a mix of Swiss and international cuisine in a stylish setting with views of

Lake Lucerne.

**Fritschi**: A popular restaurant offering Swiss comfort food, including rosti, sausages, and hearty meat dishes.

Rathaus Brauerei: A brewery restaurant selling Swiss specialties and a wide range of beers brewed on-site.

These are just a few examples of famous cafes and restaurants in Switzerland. It's advisable to check their opening hours and make reservations in advance, especially during peak seasons, to secure your chosen dining experience.

## 10.2 Regional Swiss Cuisine

Switzerland is known for its diverse regional cuisine, with each area having unique dishes and flavors. Here are some features of regional Swiss cuisine:

**Bernese Cuisine (Bern):**

Try traditional dishes like Berner Platte, a plate of different meats, sausages, and smoked pork served with sauerkraut and potatoes.

Sample the iconic Bernese specialty, Rösti, a Swiss-style grated and fried potato dish often served as a side or a main meal.

**Appenzell Cuisine (Appenzell):**

Appenzeller cheese is a popular local specialty. Enjoy it in recipes like Älplermagronen, a hearty pasta and cheese dish.

Taste the traditional Appenzeller sausage, a flavorful and

spiced sausage that goes well with regional cheeses.

**Valais Cuisine (Valais)**:

Discover the flavors of Valais with dishes like Raclette, a melted cheese dish usually served with potatoes, pickles, and cured meats.

Taste the famous Walliser Käseschnitte, a grilled cheese sandwich made with area cheeses.

**Ticino Cuisine (Ticino)**:

Ticino is inspired by Italian cuisine, with dishes like Risotto alla Milanese, a saffron-infused risotto.

Polenta is a staple in Ticino, often served with hearty soups or accompanied by local cheeses and mushrooms.

Graubünden Cuisine (Graubünden):

Sample Bündnerfleisch, air-dried beef served thinly sliced as a cold meat treat.

Try Capuns, an area specialty made from Swiss chard or spinach leaves stuffed with a filling of meat, herbs, and spices.

**Lake Geneva Region Cuisine**:

Explore the flavors of Lake Geneva with meals like Filets de Perche, breaded and fried perch fillets, often served with fries and tartar sauce.

Enjoy Papet Vaudois, a classic dish of leeks and potatoes cooked with sausage, served with mustard sauce.

**Basel Cuisine (Basel):**

Taste the classic Basel specialty, Basler Läckerli, a spiced gingerbread biscuit made with honey, nuts, and candied peel.

Try Zwiebelkuchen, a savory onion tart made with a yeast dough and eaten during the harvest season.

These are just a few examples of the regional Swiss cuisine you can study. Each area offers its own culinary delights, showcasing local ingredients and customs. Make sure to indulge in the specialties of the area you visit to truly experience the rich flavors of Swiss food.

## 10.3 Vegetarian and Vegan Options

Switzerland has a growing number of vegetarian and vegan-friendly places that cater to the dietary preferences of plant-based eaters. Here are some choices for vegetarian and vegan dining in Switzerland:

**Hiltl (Zurich):**

Hiltl is the world's oldest vegetarian restaurant, offering a wide range of plant-based meals.

Enjoy a variety of vegetarian and vegan choices, including salads, curries, stir-fries, and desserts.

**Tibits (Various locations):**

Tibits is a popular vegetarian and vegan buffet-style restaurant with multiple sites across Switzerland.

You can choose from a diverse selection of hot and cold meals, salads, soups, and desserts.

**Vegelateria (Zurich):**

Vegelateria is a vegan gelato shop that offers a delightful array of plant-based ice cream tastes.

Enjoy a refreshing treat with tastes like chocolate,

strawberry, coconut, and more.

**Kafi für Dich (Bern):**

Kafi für Dich is a cozy café in Bern that offers a range of vegetarian and vegan options.

Indulge in their delicious plant-based food items, sandwiches, soups, and baked goods.

**Veganista (Zurich):**

Veganista is a vegan fast-food restaurant in Zurich, serving up tasty burgers, wraps, and salads.

They offer a range of plant-based alternatives to classic fast-food dishes.

**Roots (Geneva):**

Roots is a vegan café and restaurant in Geneva, specializing in healthy and delicious plant-based food.

Enjoy their unique salads, bowls, wraps, and desserts, all made with fresh and natural ingredients.

**Vegan Kitchen (Lausanne):**

Vegan Kitchen is a popular vegan restaurant in Lausanne, having a diverse menu of plant-based dishes.

Their menu features international flavors and includes choices such as burgers, wraps, pasta, and desserts.

**Daizy (Lucerne):**

Daizy is a vegetarian and vegan café in Lucerne, known for its flavorful and nutritious plant-based meals.

Enjoy their fresh salads, sandwiches, smoothie bowls, and vegan sweets.

These are just a few examples of vegetarian and vegan-friendly businesses in Switzerland. In addition to specialized vegetarian and vegan restaurants, many mainstream restaurants and cafés also offer vegetarian and vegan options on their menus. When dining out, it's always a good idea to tell the staff about your dietary preferences to ensure you are served suitable options.

## 10.4 Food Festivals and Markets

Switzerland hosts various food festivals and markets throughout the year, showcasing local and foreign culinary delights. Attending these events allows you to immerse yourself in the vibrant food culture and find new flavors. Here are some famous food festivals and markets in Switzerland:

**Street Food Festival (Various locations)**:

This traveling food festival showcases a wide range of international street food vendors, giving flavors from around the world.

Explore the various food stalls, try different cuisines, and enjoy live music and entertainment.

**Fête de l'Escalade (Geneva)**:

This historic festival marks the city's victory over an invasion in the 17th century.

Along with traditional parades and reenactments, the event features food stalls offering Escalade specialties like vegetable soup, mulled wine, and chocolates.

**Zürcher Weinland Wine and Food Festival (Zurich)**:

Held in the scenic Zürcher Weinland region, this event

celebrates local wines and regional culinary delights.

Sample wines from nearby vineyards, taste traditional Swiss dishes, and enjoy live music and entertainment.

### Slow Food Market (Bern):

This annual event supports sustainable and locally produced food.

Explore a variety of stalls selling organic produce, artisanal cheeses, bread, chocolate, and other specialty products.

### Montreux Christmas Market (Montreux):

During the holiday season, Montreux hosts a charming Christmas market.

Discover a wide range of seasonal treats, including Swiss chocolates, gingerbread, roasted chestnuts, and mulled wine.

### Vevey Winegrowers Festival (Vevey):

This once-in-a-generation festival celebrates the wine culture of the area.

Enjoy food stalls selling regional specialties, live music, parades, and traditional performances.

### Bellinzona Market (Bellinzona):

Bellinzona's weekly market offers a vibrant atmosphere and a range of local products.

Explore stalls offering fresh fruits, vegetables, cheese, cured meats, pastries, and regional delicacies.

### Chur Street Food Festival (Chur):

This street food event gathers a diverse range of vendors, giving culinary delights from various cuisines.

Discover an array of delicious street food choices, from gourmet burgers to Asian fusion dishes.

These are just a few examples of the food events and markets in Switzerland. The dates and locations of these events may change from year to year, so it's advisable to check the latest information and schedules before planning your visit. Participating in these events and markets is a great way to experience the local food scene, indulge in delicious treats, and immerse yourself in Swiss culinary culture.

## 10.5 Wine and Swiss Spirits

Switzerland is known for its excellent wines and traditional spirits, giving a diverse range of flavors and varieties. Exploring Swiss wines and spirits allows you to learn the country's rich viticulture and distillation customs. Here are some features of Swiss wines and spirits:

**Swiss Wines**:

Switzerland produces a variety of wines, with each region having unique flavors and grape varietals.

Explore the wineries of Valais, Vaud, Geneva, and Ticino to taste local wines such as Chasselas, Pinot Noir, Gamay, and Merlot.

Visit wineries for tastings and tours to learn about the winemaking process and the unique qualities of Swiss wines.

**Fendant**:

Fendant is a popular white wine made in the Valais region.

Made from the Chasselas grape, Fendant is known for its crispness, lightness, and fruity notes.

It goes well with Swiss cheeses, seafood, and light dishes.

**Swiss Spirits**:

Switzerland has a history of producing fine spirits, including fruit brandies, liqueurs, and absinthe.

Try the traditional Swiss spirit "Williamine," a pear brandy made from Williams pears.

Explore Swiss herbal liqueurs like "Appenzeller Alpenbitter" and "Engelberg Kräuterliqueur" known for their aromatic and herbal tastes.

**Swiss Whisky**:

Switzerland has also entered the world of whisky production, with distilleries creating their own unique expressions.

Discover Swiss single malt whiskies, aged in a range of cask types, and discover the flavors influenced by the local terroir.

**Aperitifs**:

Switzerland is known for its aperitif culture, with famous drinks like "Vermouth" and "Zuger Kirsch" (cherry liqueur).

Enjoy a famous Swiss aperitif by sipping Vermouth on the rocks or try a "Kirsch-Cola" for a refreshing combination of cherry liqueur and cola.

When visiting Switzerland, try taking part in wine tastings at local wineries or exploring specialty shops to sample Swiss wines and spirits. Many cities and towns have wine bars and caves where you can enjoy a glass of wine or a tasting flight. Additionally, you can find Swiss wines and drinks in restaurants, bars, and specialized shops throughout the country. Cheers to learning the flavors of Swiss wine and spirits!

# Shopping in Switzerland

## 11.1 Swiss Souvenirs and Gifts

Switzerland is renowned for its high-quality craftsmanship and iconic products, making it a great location for shopping and finding unique souvenirs and gifts. Here are some famous Swiss souvenirs and gift ideas to consider:

**Swiss Chocolate**:

Swiss chocolate is world-famous for its smooth texture and rich tastes. Look for famous Swiss chocolate brands like Lindt, Toblerone, and Sprüngli.

Visit chocolate shops and stores to choose from a variety of chocolate bars, pralines, truffles, and specialty creations.

**Swiss Watches**:

Switzerland is associated with precision timepieces and luxury watches. Consider buying a Swiss watch as a timeless and elegant gift.

Explore watch shops in major Swiss cities like Geneva, Zurich, and Lucerne to find renowned Swiss watch brands such as Rolex, Omega, TAG Heuer, and Swatch.

**Swiss Cheese**:

Bring home a taste of Switzerland by buying authentic Swiss cheeses. Popular types include Gruyère, Emmental, Appenzeller, and Tête de Moine.

Visit local cheese shops or markets to find a wide range of Swiss cheeses, often accompanied by traditional cheese-making demonstrations.

**Swiss Army Knife**:

The Swiss Army Knife is an iconic Swiss product known for its flexibility and precision. It makes for a useful and enduring souvenir.

Look for official Victorinox or Wenger Swiss Army Knives, available in various sizes and designs to fit different needs.

**Swiss Textiles and Embroidery**:

Switzerland is known for its fine textiles and detailed embroidery. Consider buying Swiss-made clothing, handkerchiefs, or table linens adorned with traditional Swiss designs.

Look for specialty shops or visit regions like St. Gallen, known for its rich textile heritage, to find a range of Swiss textiles.

**Swiss Music Boxes**:

Swiss music boxes are beautiful and charming memories. These handmade boxes often feature intricate woodwork and play traditional Swiss melodies.

Explore souvenir shops or specialty stores to find music boxes in different sizes and designs, making for a lovely gift.

**Swiss Cowbells**:

Swiss cowbells are a symbol of the country's agricultural history. These ornamental bells come in various sizes and are often adorned with traditional Swiss designs.

Look for cowbell souvenirs in gift shops or visit areas like the Bernese Oberland to find authentic cowbells.

**Swiss Posters and Art Prints**:

Switzerland is known for its stunning scenery and picturesque towns. Consider purchasing Swiss posters or art prints showing scenic views or iconic sites.

Visit local art galleries or souvenir shops to find a variety of prints catching the beauty of Switzerland.

When shopping for Swiss souvenirs and gifts, keep in mind the customs laws of your home country regarding the import of food products and other items. Also, consider helping local artisans and businesses by buying authentic Swiss products.

## 11.2 Luxury Brands and Watches\

Switzerland is synonymous with luxury and craftsmanship, especially in the realm of watches and high-end brands. If you're interested in indulging in luxury shopping experiences or seeking prestigious timepieces, Switzerland offers a wealth of choices. Here are some highlights for luxury names and watches:

Luxury Brands:
**Bahnhofstrasse, Zurich**: Known as one of the world's most exclusive shopping streets, Bahnhofstrasse is home to luxury boutiques and flagship stores of renowned names like Louis Vuitton, Chanel, Gucci, and Prada.
Rue du Rhône, Geneva: This elegant street in Geneva is lined with upscale shops, including prestigious names like Cartier, Dior, Hermès, and Rolex. It's a paradise for luxury clothes and accessories.
**Grieder, Zurich**: Located on Bahnhofstrasse, Grieder is a high-end department store offering a curated range of luxury fashion brands, including international designers and Swiss labels.

**Globus, Zurich and Geneva**: Globus is a Swiss department store chain that displays a range of luxury brands, from fashion and cosmetics to home decor and gourmet foods.

Luxury Watches:

**Watch Stores in Geneva**: Geneva is known as a hub for luxury watches. Explore watch boutiques and approved dealers to find prestigious Swiss watch brands like Patek Philippe, Audemars Piguet, Vacheron Constantin, and many others.

**Watch Stores in Zurich**: Zurich also offers a plethora of watch shops, offering both luxury Swiss brands and international watchmakers. Discover timepieces from names like Rolex, Omega, IWC, and TAG Heuer.

Baselworld Watch and Jewelry Show: If your visit overlaps with the annual Baselworld fair, you'll have the opportunity to immerse yourself in the world's largest watch and jewelry exhibition, where top luxury brands present their latest creations.

**La Chaux-de-Fonds and Le Locle**: These Swiss towns are famous for their historical connections to watchmaking. Visit watch museums, workshops, and even tour watch factories to gain insights into the craft and history of Swiss watchmaking.

When indulging in luxury shopping experiences, it's advisable to set a budget and consider your personal tastes. Take your time exploring boutiques, seek expert guidance from authorized dealers, and ensure the authenticity of the products you buy. Switzerland's luxury brands and watches reflect the country's commitment to precision, craftsmanship, and timeless elegance.

## 11.3 Traditional Crafts and Artwork

Switzerland has a rich tradition of craftsmanship and traditional arts, giving a variety of unique and authentic creations. If you're interested in studying traditional crafts and artwork, Switzerland has much to offer. Here are some highlights:

Woodcarving:

Switzerland is known for its intricate woodcarvings, especially in regions like the Bernese Oberland and Valais.

Look for handmade wooden figurines, traditional masks, cuckoo clocks, and decorative items made by skilled Swiss woodcarvers.

**Embroidery and Textiles**:

Regions like St. Gallen are famous for their exquisite embroidery and lacework.

Look for Swiss-made textiles, such as embroidered tablecloths, handkerchiefs, and traditional outfits adorned with delicate lacework.

**Pottery and Ceramics:**

Visit pottery workshops and shops in regions like Ticino, where you can find beautifully crafted ceramics with traditional Swiss designs.

Look for pottery items such as bowls, plates, vases, and decorative objects that highlight the unique regional styles.

**Papercutting**:

Swiss papercutting, known as "Scherenschnitt," is a traditional art form that includes intricate designs cut from paper.

Look for papercut artworks featuring Swiss landscapes, folklore, or symbols, which make for stunning wall decorations or framed keepsakes.

**Cowbell Art**:

Swiss cowbells, usually worn by cows grazing in the Alpine meadows, have become iconic symbols of Swiss heritage.

Look for cowbells adorned with decorative designs, intricate patterns, and engravings, often featuring traditional Swiss themes.

**Alphorn**:

The Alphorn is a traditional Swiss musical instrument made of wood, originally used by shepherds in the Alps.

Look for miniature Alphorns or decorative pieces made by skilled artisans, which can serve as unique souvenirs or decorative items.

**Swiss Folk Art**:

Swiss folk art includes a variety of traditional crafts, including painted wooden objects, glassware, and traditional costumes.

Look for items such as painted chalet-style boxes, glassware with intricate designs, or dolls dressed in traditional Swiss garb.

When looking for traditional crafts and artwork, try visiting local artisans, craft markets, or specialty shops. These locations provide chances to meet the artists, learn about their techniques, and purchase authentic Swiss creations. Supporting traditional crafts helps protect Swiss cultural heritage and ensures the continuation of these artistic traditions for future generations.

## 11.4 Swiss Chocolate and Confectionery

Switzerland is renowned internationally for its exquisite chocolate and confectionery. Swiss chocolate is known for its smooth texture, rich flavors, and careful craftsmanship. If you're a chocolate lover or looking for delectable treats to bring back as gifts, Switzerland offers an array of choices. Here are some samples of Swiss chocolate and confectionery:

**Swiss Chocolate Brands**:

Lindt: Lindt is a popular Swiss chocolate brand known for its smooth, melt-in-your-mouth chocolate. Look for their famous Lindor truffles and assorted chocolate bars.

**Toblerone**: Toblerone is known for its unique triangular shape and honey-almond nougat flavor. It's an iconic Swiss chocolate brand available in different sizes and flavors.

**Sprüngli**: Sprüngli, based in Zurich, is famous for its luxurious pralines and truffles. Indulge in their famous "Luxemburgerli" macarons and handmade chocolate creations.

Chocolate Shops and Boutiques:

**Confiserie Teuscher (Zurich):** This famous chocolatier offers a wide selection of handmade truffles, pralines, and chocolate specialties, including their signature Champagne truffles.

**Läderach (Various locations):** Läderach is known for its high-quality Swiss chocolate, especially their FrischSchoggi (fresh chocolate) made with premium ingredients and creative flavors.

**Maison Cailler (Broc):** Visit Maison Cailler, Switzerland's oldest chocolate brand, for a delightful chocolate tour, tasting, and a chance to learn about the past of Swiss chocolate-making.

Chocolate Museums and Experiences:

**Maison Cailler (Broc)**: Explore the engaging exhibits at Maison Cailler, where you can learn about the chocolate-making process, taste samples, and discover the secrets of Swiss chocolate.

**Swiss Chocolate Chalet (Gruyères)**: Immerse yourself in the world of chocolate at the Swiss Chocolate Chalet, where you can learn about Swiss chocolate traditions, join in workshops, and indulge in tastings.

Confectionery Delights:

**Nougat**: Swiss nougat, made with honey, nuts, and

sometimes chocolate, is a famous sweet treat. Look for nougat bars or nougat-filled candies for a delightful confectionery experience.

**Swiss Truffles**: Swiss truffles are delicate chocolate ganache balls covered in cocoa powder or chocolate shavings. They come in different flavors, such as dark chocolate, milk chocolate, and fruity variations.

When looking for Swiss chocolate and confectionery, you can find a wide range in local grocery stores, souvenir shops, and specialized chocolate boutiques. Look for beautifully packaged gift boxes or build your own assortment of chocolates to enjoy or share with friends and family. Swiss chocolate and confectionery make for delectable treats and delightful souvenirs that catch the essence of Switzerland's sweet indulgence.

# Practical Information

## 12.1 Local Customs and Etiquette

Switzerland has its own set of customs and etiquette that tourists should be aware of to ensure a pleasant and respectful experience. Here are some key things to keep in mind:

**Punctuality**: Swiss people value punctuality, so it's

important to be on time for meetings, appointments, and social events. Being late is generally seen as rude.

Greetings: When meeting someone for the first time, a firm handshake and direct eye contact are usual. Swiss people usually address others using their last names unless invited to use first names.

**Politeness**: Swiss culture values politeness and courtesy. It is usual to say "please" (bitte) and "thank you" (danke) when interacting with others. Simple greetings like "good morning" (guten Morgen) and "good evening" (guten Abend) are also welcomed.

**Respect for Personal Space**: Swiss people value personal space, so it's important to keep a reasonable distance when conversing. Avoid touching or hugging someone unless you have a close friendship.

**Dress Code**: Swiss people usually dress neatly and conservatively. For most situations, casual or business casual attire is acceptable. However, if you plan to visit upscale restaurants, theaters, or events, smart casual or formal attire may be needed.

**Smoking Regulations**: Switzerland has strict regulations surrounding smoking. Smoking is usually prohibited in public indoor areas, including restaurants, bars, and public transportation. Look for designated smoking areas or ask for advice if you need to smoke.

**Noise and Quiet Hours**: Swiss cities and towns often have set quiet hours during the evening and nighttime. It is respectful to keep noise levels low during these hours, especially in residential areas and hotels.

**Recycling and Waste Disposal**: Switzerland has a strong dedication to recycling and waste management. Be mindful of separating and disposing of your waste according to the unique recycling guidelines in your area. Many public places have recycling bins available
.

By respecting local customs and etiquette, you can show appreciation for Swiss culture and create good interactions with locals. Remember that customs may vary slightly depending on the area or city you're visiting, so it's always helpful to observe and follow the behavior of the locals.

## 12.2 Language Phrases and Translations

Switzerland is a bilingual country, with four official languages: German, French, Italian, and Romansh. The language spoken in each region varies, so it's helpful to learn a few basic phrases in the local language of the place you're visiting. Here are some popular phrases and their translations:

German (Swiss German):

Hello: Grüezi

Goodbye: Tschüss/Auf Wiedersehen

Thank you: Danke

Please: Bitte
Yes: Ja
No: Nein
Excuse me: Entschuldigung
Do you understand English?: Sprechen Sie Englisch?
I don't understand: Ich verstehe nicht
Where is...?: Wo ist...?
How much does it cost?: Wie viel kostet das?
French:
Hello: Bonjour
Goodbye: Au revoir
Thank you: Merci
Please: S'il vous plaît
Yes: Oui
No: Non
Excuse me: Excusez-moi
Do you understand English?: Parlez-vous anglais?
I don't understand: Je ne comprends pas
Where is...?: Où se trouve...?
How much does it cost?: Combien ça coûte?
Italian:
Hello: Buongiorno
Goodbye: Arrivederci
Thank you: Grazie
Please: Per favore
Yes: Sì
No: No
Excuse me: Mi scusi

Do you understand English?: Parla inglese?

I don't understand: Non capisco

Where is...?: Dove si trova...?

How much does it cost?: Quanto costa?

Romansh:

Hello: Bun di/Buna sera

Goodbye: Adia/Schau

Thank you: Grazia fitg

Please: Per plaschair

Yes: Tess

No: Na

Excuse me: Excusa

Do you understand English?: Tgiesas englais?

I don't understand: Na chapeschai betg

Where is...?: U sa...?

How much does it cost?: Quanto custa quai?

These are just a few simple phrases to get you started. It's always appreciated when visitors make an effort to converse in the local language. However, English is widely spoken in tourist areas, so if you face any language barriers, don't hesitate to ask if someone speaks English. Swiss people are generally friendly and accommodating.

## 12.3 Tipping and Service Charges

Tipping methods in Switzerland are different from those in some other countries. Here are some rules regarding tipping and service charges:

**Restaurants and Cafés**:

In Swiss restaurants, a service charge is often included in the bill. Look for "Service compris" or "Service inbegriffen" on the menu or ticket.

If a service charge is included, it's not mandatory to leave an extra tip. However, rounding up the bill or leaving a small amount as a gesture of appreciation is usual.

If a service charge is not included, a tip of around 5-10% of the total price is appreciated for good service. You can give the tip straight to the waiter or leave it on the table when paying.

**Bars and Cafés**:

In bars and cafés, it's normal to round up the bill as a tip. For example, if your bill is CHF 4.50, you can round it up to CHF 5.

If you receive table service in a café or bar, you can leave a small tip of around 5% of the total bill.

**Taxis**:

It's usual to round up the fare when taking a taxi. For example, if your price is CHF 17.60, you can round it up to CHF 18.

If the taxi driver provides exceptional service or helps with luggage, you can give a slightly higher tip as a token of gratitude.

**Hotel Staff**:

Tipping hotel staff is not mandatory, but it's common to

leave a small tip for services given.

You can tip the hotel porter who helps with your luggage, housekeeping staff who clean your room, and the concierge for their assistance.

It's usual to leave CHF 1-2 per bag for the porter and CHF 2-5 per day for the housekeeping staff.

**Other Services:**

For other services, such as hairdressers, tour guides, or spa treatments, it's common to leave a tip of around 5-10% of the service cost, based on the quality of service received.

It's important to note that tipping is a personal choice and should be based on your satisfaction with the service given. If you feel that the service was exceptional or went above and beyond your standards, you can leave a more generous tip. However, tipping should never be seen as an obligation and should always be given as a token of thanks for good service.


## 12.4 Public Holidays and Store Hours

Switzerland observes several public holidays throughout the year, and store hours may change on these days. Here are some of the big public holidays in Switzerland and information about store hours:

**New Year's Day (Neujahrstag) - January 1st**:

Public holiday. Most shops and businesses are closed on this day.

Good Friday (Karfreitag) - Friday before Easter Sunday:
Public holiday. Many stores and businesses are closed, although some tourist areas and bigger cities may have limited store openings.

Easter Monday (Ostermontag) - Monday following Easter Sunday:
Public holiday. Most shops and businesses are closed on this day.

Ascension Day (Auffahrt) - 39 days after Easter Sunday:
Public holiday. Most shops and businesses are closed on this day.

Whit Monday (Pfingstmontag) - Monday following Pentecost Sunday:
Public holiday. Many stores and businesses are closed, although some tourist areas and bigger cities may have limited store openings.

Swiss National Day (Schweizer Bundesfeiertag) - August 1st:
Public holiday. Most shops and businesses are closed on this day.

Christmas Day (Weihnachtstag) - December 25th:
Public holiday. All shops and businesses are closed on this day.

St. Stephen's Day (Stephanstag) - December 26th:
Public holiday. Most shops and businesses are closed on this day.

Note: Canton-specific holidays may also change store hours in certain regions.

**Store Hours:**

Normal store hours in Switzerland are usually from Monday to Friday, 9:00 AM to 6:30 PM, and Saturdays from 9:00 AM to 4:00 PM.

Some bigger cities, such as Zurich and Geneva, may have extended store hours on Thursdays until 8:00 PM.

Grocery shops in urban areas may have longer opening hours, with some staying open until 8:00 PM or later, including Saturdays.

Sunday store openings are limited in Switzerland, and most shops are closed. Exceptions include shops at airports, train stops, and tourist areas, as well as some bakeries and convenience stores.

It's important to note that store hours can vary based on the location, especially in smaller towns or rural areas. It's advisable to check the specific store's website or contact them personally for accurate information on opening hours, especially during holidays or on Sundays.

## 12.5 Internet and Wi-Fi Access

Switzerland gives reliable internet connectivity and Wi-Fi access in most areas, including cities, towns, and tourist destinations. Here's some information on getting the internet and Wi-Fi during your visit:

**Mobile Data**:

If you have a mobile phone with an active data plan, you

can use mobile data services offered by Swiss telecom operators like Swisscom, Salt, and Sunrise. Check with your mobile service provider about foreign roaming options and costs.

Switzerland has great mobile network coverage, including 4G and 5G networks, allowing you to stay connected while on the go.

**Wi-Fi Hotspots**:

Many hotels, restaurants, cafes, and public places give free Wi-Fi hotspots. Look for signs showing Wi-Fi availability or ask the staff for the network name (SSID) and password.

Major towns, such as Zurich, Geneva, and Basel, often have free public Wi-Fi networks in certain areas. These networks may require registration or acceptance of terms and conditions to join.

**Swisscom Public Wi-Fi**:

Swisscom, one of Switzerland's major telecom providers, offers public Wi-Fi hotspots throughout the country. These hotspots are available in various places, including train stations, airports, and major tourist areas.

To access Swisscom Public Wi-Fi, pick the network named "Swisscom" or "Swisscom_Auto_Login," follow the prompts to register (if required), and accept the terms and conditions.

**Internet Cafes**:

Internet cafes are offered in some Swiss cities and towns, offering computer access and internet services for a fee.

These can be useful if you don't have a mobile data plan or need a more extensive internet link.

**Portable Wi-Fi Devices**:

Another choice is to rent or purchase a portable Wi-Fi device, also known as a pocket Wi-Fi or Mi-Fi. These devices allow you to have your own personal Wi-Fi hotspot and connect multiple devices concurrently. Check with local providers or foreign rental services for availability and pricing.

When using public Wi-Fi networks, it's important to practice good cybersecurity habits and protect your personal information. Avoid accessing sensitive accounts or entering sensitive information while connecting to public Wi-Fi. Consider using a virtual private network (VPN) for an extra layer of security.

Overall, keeping connected in Switzerland is convenient, with various options available to access the internet and Wi-Fi during your visit

## 12.6 Postal Services

Switzerland has a well-developed postal system that offers reliable and efficient postal services. Whether you need to send mail or receive packages during your visit, here's some information about postal services in Switzerland:

**Swiss Post (Die Schweizerische Post):**

Swiss Post is the national postal service in Switzerland and runs post offices throughout the country.

Post offices offer a range of services, including sending letters, packages, and registered mail, as well as buying stamps and other postal products.

You can find Swiss Post offices in most towns and cities, and they are easily recognizable by their unique yellow logo.

**Postal Services**:

Sending Mail: You can send letters and postcards from Swiss Post stations. Postal rates vary based on the weight, size, and destination of the item. You can buy stamps at post offices or other authorized retailers.

Receiving Mail: If you're staying in Switzerland for an extended time, you may have mail or packages brought to your address. Postal workers will usually deliver mail directly to your mailbox or leave a notification if a package needs to be picked up from the local post office.

**Post Office Opening Hours**:

Post office opening hours may vary depending on the location, but most post offices are open from Monday to Friday, typically from 8:00 AM or 8:30 AM until 5:00 PM or 6:30 PM.

Some post offices may also have limited Saturday hours, especially in larger cities and tourist areas. It's advisable to check the individual post office's opening hours in your area.

**Additional Postal Services**:

Swiss Post gives various additional services, including express mail, international shipping, and additional insurance for valuable items.

You can inquire about specific services and rates at the post office or visit the Swiss Post website for more information.

**Poste Restante**:

If you need to receive mail or packages while moving in Switzerland, you can use the "Poste Restante" service. This service allows you to have mail sent to a post office in a specific place, where you can collect it by presenting identification. Inform the sender to address the mail as follows: "Your Name, Poste Restante, Post Office Name, Postal Code, City, Switzerland."

Swiss Post is known for its efficiency and reliability, making it a convenient choice for postal services during your stay in Switzerland. If you have any specific questions or require more information, the staff at the post offices will be happy to help you.

# Day Trips and Excursions

## 13.1 Château de Gruyères

Château de Gruyères is a captivating medieval castle situated in the picturesque town of Gruyères in the Fribourg canton of Switzerland. This historic castle is a must-visit attraction, offering a fascinating glimpse into Switzerland's rich past and providing stunning panoramic views of the surrounding countryside. Here's what you can expect from a day trip to Château de Gruyères:

**Castle Exploration**:
Step back in time as you experience the medieval halls, chambers, and courtyards of Château de Gruyères. Marvel at the well-preserved architecture and immerse yourself in the castle's charming ambiance.
Admire the intricate tapestries, ornate furniture, and

centuries-old artworks presented throughout the castle. Learn about the noble families who once resided here and the castle's historical importance.

**The Museum of Gruyères:**

Within the castle, you'll find the Museum of Gruyères, which shows the region's cultural heritage. Explore exhibits that delve into the traditions, crafts, and everyday life of the people who lived in the area throughout the centuries.

Discover the history of cheese production in the region and learn about the world-famous Gruyère cheese, for which the town is known. Gain insights into the traditional ways of cheese-making and the importance of agriculture in the local economy.

**Scenic Views:**

From the castle's towers and ramparts, soak in the breathtaking panoramic views of the nearby Swiss countryside. Take in the rolling hills, lush green fields, and the charm of the medieval town below.

Capture memorable photos of the castle's impressive exterior and the picturesque landscape that goes as far as the eye can see.

**Gruyères Town:**

After viewing the castle, take some time to wander through the charming town of Gruyères. Stroll along its cobbled streets lined with traditional Swiss houses, boutique shops, and welcoming cafes.

Indulge in a taste of the local culinary favorites. Don't

miss the chance to savor a creamy fondue, sample Swiss chocolates, or enjoy a delicious cheese platter featuring the famous Gruyère cheese.

**The HR Giger Museum (Optional):**

For fans of the famous Swiss artist HR Giger, the HR Giger Museum is located in Gruyères. This museum houses an extensive collection of Giger's unique and surreal artworks, including his famous creation, the "Alien" creature from the movie series.

Château de Gruyères offers a captivating mix of history, art, and stunning natural scenery. Immerse yourself in the medieval atmosphere, learn about Swiss culture and customs, and indulge in the culinary delights of the area. A day trip to Château de Gruyères offers an enriching and memorable experience.

## 13.2 Schaffhausen and Stein am Rhein

A day trip to Schaffhausen and Stein am Rhein will take you on a journey through beautiful towns filled with historic charm and natural beauty. Located in northern Switzerland, near the German border, these two destinations offer a delightful mix of architectural treasures, scenic landscapes, and cultural experiences. Here's what you can explore during your day trip:

**Schaffhausen:**

Start your day in Schaffhausen, a charming town known for its well-preserved old town and the magnificent

Rhine Falls, Europe's biggest waterfall.

Explore the old town, defined by its narrow streets, colorful houses, and impressive buildings. Visit the Munot Fortress, a 16th-century circular fortress with panoramic views of the city and the Rhine River.

Marvel at the architectural beauty of the All Saints' Abbey, a former Benedictine abbey that now houses the Museum zu Allerheiligen. The museum highlights regional art, history, and archaeology.

**Rhine Falls**:

Just outside Schaffhausen, a short drive or boat ride will take you to the beautiful Rhine Falls. Witness the awe-inspiring sight of the cascading waters as they plunge into the river below.

Take a boat ride to get up close to the falls or walk across the viewing decks for a panoramic view. Capture memorable pictures and enjoy the natural beauty that surrounds you.

**Stein am Rhein**:

From Schaffhausen, continue your day trip to the nearby town of Stein am Rhein, located on the banks of the Rhine River. This medieval town is famous for its well-preserved half-timbered houses adorned with lively frescoes.

Take a leisurely walk through the town's narrow streets, admiring the intricate facades and charming details of the buildings. Explore the main square, Rathausplatz, and visit the town's famous landmarks, including the

Rathaus (Town Hall) and the St. George's Abbey.

**Museum Lindwurm**:

In Stein am Rhein, you can visit the Museum Lindwurm, which displays the history and art of the town. Discover artifacts, paintings, and exhibitions that highlight the cultural heritage of the area.

**Rhine River Cruise (Optional):**

Consider taking a relaxing boat ride along the Rhine River. Enjoy the scenic views, including wineries, castles, and picturesque landscapes. Cruises often depart from Schaffhausen or Stein am Rhein, giving a unique perspective of the area.

Both Schaffhausen and Stein am Rhein offer a captivating mix of history, natural beauty, and architectural splendor. From the impressive Rhine Falls to the charming streets of Stein am Rhein, this day trip offers a delightful exploration of northern Switzerland's treasures.

## 13.3 Mount Titlis

A day trip to Mount Titlis will take you on an unforgettable alpine adventure, offering breathtaking views, exciting activities, and a chance to experience the beauty of the Swiss Alps. Here's what you can expect during your visit to Mount Titlis:

**Scenic Cable Car Ride**:

Start your trip by taking a scenic cable car ride from

Engelberg to Mount Titlis. As you ascend, enjoy panoramic views of the surrounding alpine landscapes, including snow-capped peaks, lush valleys, and picturesque Swiss towns.

**Rotair, the World's First Revolving Cable Car**:
Once you reach the top, you'll experience the unique Rotair, the world's first revolving cable car. The rotating cabin offers 360-degree views, allowing you to fully immerse yourself in the stunning mountain scenery.

**Cliff Walk**:
Embark on a thrilling adventure by crossing the famous Cliff Walk, Europe's highest suspension bridge. Suspended above a sheer drop, this adrenaline-pumping experience offers awe-inspiring views of the nearby glaciers and mountains.

**Ice Flyer Chairlift**:
Take a ride on the Ice Flyer chairlift, which takes you over the glacier's crevasses. Marvel at the icy scenery and get up close to the glacier's impressive formations.

**Glacier Cave**:
Explore the interesting Glacier Cave, an underground ice palace carved into the heart of the glacier. Admire the intricate ice sculptures and learn about the glacier's formation and importance.

**Titlis Glacier Park:**
For those seeking adventure, visit the Titlis Glacier Park, where you can enjoy snow sports such as snow tubing, sledding, and skiing. Rent equipment on-site and enjoy

the winter wonderland.

**Panoramic Views**:

From various vantage points on Mount Titlis, soak in the breathtaking panoramic views of the surrounding peaks, including the famous Matterhorn, Jungfrau, and Eiger mountains.

Capture memorable shots of the alpine scenery and the glistening snow-covered peaks.

**Alpine Dining**:

Refuel and indulge in delicious Swiss food at one of the mountain restaurants or cafes. Enjoy classic dishes like fondue, raclette, or hearty alpine specialties while enjoying the stunning views.

**Shopping and Souvenirs**:

Browse the souvenir shops and boutiques on Mount Titlis, where you can find unique Swiss souvenirs, chocolates, traditional clothing, and other memorabilia to remember your visit.

Mount Titlis offers a remarkable alpine experience with its stunning views, thrilling activities, and opportunities for relaxation and exploration. Prepare for a day filled with natural beauty, adventure, and unforgettable moments in the heart of the Swiss Alps.

## 13.4 The Swiss Riviera (Montreux, Vevey, and Lausanne)

A day trip to the Swiss Riviera will transport you to the picturesque shores of Lake Geneva, where you can experience the charming towns of Montreux, Vevey, and Lausanne. Known for their stunning lakeside settings, cultural richness, and delightful culinary experiences, these places offer a perfect blend of natural beauty and vibrant city life. Here's what you can discover during your visit to the Swiss Riviera:

**Montreux**:

Begin your day in Montreux, a famous resort town nestled on the shores of Lake Geneva. Stroll along the scenic lakeside promenade, lined with palm trees and adorned with flowers, and take in the breathtaking views of the lake and nearby mountains.

Visit the famous Château de Chillon, a medieval castle perched on a rocky outcrop near Montreux. Explore its ancient halls, courtyards, and towers while learning about its fascinating past.

Explore the Montreux Jazz Festival grounds, located near the waterfront, and immerse yourself in the rich musical history of the area.

Don't miss the Freddie Mercury Statue, a tribute to the legendary singer who loved Montreux and recorded many songs at the Mountain Studios. It's a favorite spot for fans and music enthusiasts.

**Vevey:**

Just a short distance from Montreux, Vevey is another charming town that oozes old-world charm and beauty. Take a leisurely walk along the lakeside promenade and enjoy the views of the lake and the nearby vineyards.

Visit the Chaplin's World museum, dedicated to the life and work of Charlie Chaplin, the famous silent film actor. Explore his former home, see memorabilia, and learn about his extraordinary career.

Discover the Alimentarium, a fascinating museum devoted to food, nutrition, and gastronomy. Dive into the world of food through interactive exhibits, classes, and tastings.

**Lausanne:**

Continue your day trip to Lausanne, the vibrant city of the Vaud canton. Explore the steep, winding streets of the old town, known as the "Cité," and enjoy its well-preserved medieval architecture.

Visit the majestic Lausanne Cathedral, a gem of Gothic architecture, and climb its tower for panoramic views of the city and Lake Geneva.

Explore the Olympic Museum, located on the banks of Lake Geneva, and delve into the past of the Olympic Games through engaging exhibits, interactive displays, and memorabilia.

Take a leisurely walk along the Ouchy promenade, enjoy the lakeside atmosphere, and stop by the picturesque Ouchy Marina.

**Gastronomic Delights**:
Indulge in the culinary wonders of the Swiss Riviera. Taste exquisite Swiss chocolates, enjoy local wines, and experience the region's gastronomic treasures. Explore the local markets, cafes, and restaurants, and savor the flavors of Swiss food.

The Swiss Riviera offers a delightful mix of natural beauty, cultural heritage, and gastronomic experiences. Immerse yourself in the charm of Montreux, Vevey, and Lausanne, and enjoy the peaceful ambiance of Lake Geneva. Whether you're captivated by history, music, art, or simply the stunning surroundings, a day trip to the Swiss Riviera offers an enriching and memorable experience.

## 13.5 The Lavaux Vineyards

A day trip to the Lavaux Vineyards will take you to one of Switzerland's most picturesque wine regions, known for its terraced vineyards, stunning lake views, and rich viticultural heritage. Located on the shores of Lake Geneva between Lausanne and Vevey, the Lavaux Vineyards offer a unique mix of natural beauty, cultural significance, and wine appreciation. Here's what you can explore during your visit to the Lavaux Vineyards:
**Scenic Vineyard Walks**:
Embark on a leisurely walk through the terraced

vineyards, following the well-marked paths that wind their way through the picturesque landscapes. Enjoy breathtaking views of Lake Geneva, the Alps, and the nearby vine-covered slopes.

Marvel at the precision and workmanship of the vineyard terraces, which are recognized as a UNESCO World Heritage site. Learn about the viticultural methods and the region's rich winemaking traditions.

**Wine Tastings and Cellar Visits**:

Discover the local wineries and enjoy wine tastings of the region's famous white wines, especially Chasselas, which is the most prominent grape variety in Lavaux.

Visit the wine cellars and learn about the winemaking process from the enthusiastic local winemakers. Gain insights into the unique terroir, grape varieties, and the art of wine production in the area.

**Wine Museums and Interpretive Centers**:

Explore the wine museums and interpretive centers scattered throughout the Lavaux area. These institutions offer interactive exhibits, educational displays, and multimedia presentations that dig into the history, culture, and significance of winemaking in Lavaux.

Discover the techniques of wine production, the role of the vineyards in shaping the landscape, and the social and economic aspects of the local wine business.

**Wine and Gastronomy Experiences**:

Enhance your visit by indulging in wine and gastronomy adventures. Enjoy meals or snacks at local wineries, where you can pair the wines with regional favorites and traditional Swiss dishes.

Join organized wine tours or workshops that allow you to expand your knowledge of wine tasting, food pairing, and the nuances of Lavaux wines.

**Lake Geneva Boat Cruise**:

Consider combining your visit to the Lavaux Vineyards with a boat tour on Lake Geneva. Cruise along the lake's scenic shores, taking in the beauty of the vineyards from a different viewpoint. Some cruises offer guided commentary on the region's wine production and cultural history.

The Lavaux Vineyards offer a serene and picturesque setting, where you can immerse yourself in the world of winemaking, explore the beautiful landscapes, and savor the flavors of the region's wines. Discover the allure of this UNESCO-recognized wine area and respect the harmonious blend of nature, culture, and viticulture that defines the Lavaux experience.

## 13.6 The Glacier Express

Embark on an extraordinary trip aboard the Glacier Express, one of the world's most scenic train rides. This iconic railway path spans 291 kilometers, winding through the Swiss Alps, and offers breathtaking views of snow-capped mountains, lush valleys, and charming Alpine towns. Here's what you can expect during your

Glacier Express adventure:

**Scenic Train Ride:**

Board the luxurious panoramic train and settle into comfortable seats with large windows that provide unobstructed views of the stunning scenery along the way.

Relax and enjoy the leisurely pace as the train winds its way through tunnels, over viaducts, and across bridges, showing awe-inspiring vistas at every turn.

Marvel at the changing scenery, from deep gorges to idyllic fields, from towering peaks to picturesque Alpine lakes.

**Iconic Landmarks:**

Pass by iconic sights such as the Landwasser Viaduct, a UNESCO World Heritage site known for its striking architecture, and the Rhine Gorge, also called the "Swiss Grand Canyon," with its dramatic cliffs and the roaring Rhine River.

Admire the enchanting beauty of the Andermatt region, the Oberalp Pass, and the captivating village of Zermatt with the iconic Matterhorn as its background.

**Comfort and Service:**

The Glacier Express offers excellent onboard service, including multilingual staff who can provide information about the route, landmarks, and places of interest.

Enjoy the comfort of spacious seating, and enjoy culinary delights served at your seat or in the onboard restaurant car. Indulge in regional specialties and Swiss food while gazing at the breathtaking views outside.

**Opportunities for Exploration**:

Along the way, the Glacier Express makes stops at various picturesque towns and Alpine resorts. You can choose to break your journey and discover these charming destinations, including Zermatt, Brig, Andermatt, Chur, and St. Moritz.

Discover the unique character of each town, visit their historical sites, enjoy outdoor activities, and immerse yourself in the beauty of the Swiss Alps.

**Traveling in Comfort and Style**:

The Glacier Express offers different classes of service, including standard class, first class, and even luxurious Excellence Class, ensuring that you can choose the level of comfort and amenities that suit your tastes and budget. The Glacier Express is a truly memorable experience, offering an enchanting and immersive journey through the Swiss Alps. Whether you start on the full trip from Zermatt to St. Moritz or choose a shorter segment, the breathtaking landscapes, comfortable accommodations, and impeccable service will make your Glacier Express adventure an unforgettable one.

# Sustainable Tourism in Switzerland

## 14.1 Eco-friendly Practices and Initiatives

Switzerland is committed to promoting sustainable tourism and protecting its natural beauty for future generations. The country has adopted various eco-friendly practices and initiatives to minimize the environmental impact of tourism. Here are some examples of sustainable tourism activities in Switzerland:

**Cycling and Walking**:

Switzerland offers an extensive network of cycling and walking trails, allowing guests to explore the country's scenic landscapes in an environmentally friendly way. Many cities and towns have bike-sharing programs, and walking tours are available to discover local sites on foot.

**Sustainable Accommodations**:

The country encourages eco-friendly accommodations that value energy efficiency, waste reduction, and water conservation. Look for accommodations that have received sustainability certifications such as the Swiss "Eco-label" or "Minergie" certification, showing their commitment to environmental responsibility.

**Waste Management**:

Switzerland has a well-developed waste management system, stressing recycling, composting, and proper waste disposal. Visitors are urged to follow recycling rules and dispose of waste responsibly.

**Protected Areas and National Parks**:

Switzerland has several protected areas and national parks that maintain its unique ecosystems and biodiversity. Visitors are urged to respect the rules and guidelines of these protected areas, ensuring minimal disturbance to the natural environment.

**Renewable Energy**:

Switzerland is known for its dedication to renewable energy sources. Many accommodations, attractions, and public buildings utilize renewable energy technologies such as solar power and hydropower, reducing their carbon footprint.

**Sustainable Dining**:

Swiss cuisine emphasizes local and seasonal ingredients, reducing the carbon footprint involved with long-distance transportation. Restaurants often serve dishes made from locally sourced produce, supporting local farmers and minimizing environmental effect.

**Nature Conservation Projects**:

Switzerland actively supports nature conservation projects and efforts. Visitors can join in activities such as wildlife monitoring, habitat restoration, or volunteer programs to help to the preservation of Switzerland's natural heritage.

**Responsible Outdoor Recreation**:

Visitors are urged to engage in responsible outdoor

activities, respecting wildlife, ecosystems, and fragile environments. Stick to designated trails, avoid disturbing wildlife, and follow "Leave No Trace" ideals by minimizing waste and leaving nature as you found it.

By promoting eco-friendly practices and initiatives, Switzerland aims to ensure a sustainable future for its tourism business. Visitors can actively contribute to these efforts by making environmentally aware choices and embracing the country's commitment to preserving its natural beauty.

## 14.2 Responsible Outdoor Activities

Switzerland's stunning landscapes offer a plethora of outdoor sports for guests to enjoy responsibly. Engaging in these activities with an environmentally friendly attitude helps preserve the natural beauty of the country. Here are some examples of responsible outdoor activities you can partake in while visiting Switzerland:

**Hiking and Trekking**:

Stick to marked trails and avoid venturing into protected or sensitive areas. Follow the "Leave No Trace" principles by carrying out your trash, minimizing your effect, and respecting the natural environment.

**Cycling and Mountain Biking**:

Stick to marked cycling paths and trails, respecting pedestrians and other users. Be mindful of fragile ecosystems, and avoid off-road biking in protected places.

**Water Sports**:

When engaging in water sports like swimming, kayaking, or paddleboarding, follow local laws and respect the natural habitats. Avoid disturbing wildlife and sensitive aquatic places.

**Wildlife Viewing**:

Observe wildlife from a distance, using binoculars or zoom lenses instead of approaching or feeding them. Maintain a polite distance to avoid causing stress or harm to the animals.

**Camping and Campfires**:

Camp only in designated areas and follow camping rules. When building a campfire, use marked fire pits and ensure the fire is fully extinguished before leaving. Respect any fire limits that may be in place.

**Winter Sports**:

When skiing, snowboarding, or snowshoeing, stay on marked slopes and trails. Respect signage and safety rules to ensure your own safety and the protection of the natural environment.

**Photography and Drone Use**:

Take pictures without disturbing wildlife or their habitats. Be aware of any local regulations regarding drone use and receive the necessary permits if flying a drone.

**Responsible Fishing**:

If fishing, follow local fishing regulations and receive

the required permits. Practice catch-and-release whenever possible, and respect the habitats and fish populations.

**Respect Local Communities**:
Be considerate of local groups, their traditions, and their privacy. Follow any guidelines or restrictions in place, particularly in rural or residential areas.

**Environmental Education and Conservation**:
Take the chance to learn about the local ecosystems, wildlife, and conservation efforts. Participate in educational programs or support local conservation groups to contribute to the preservation of the natural environment.

By engaging in responsible outdoor activities, you can minimize your impact on the environment and help protect the beauty of Switzerland's landscapes for future generations. Remember to always prioritize the protection of nature, follow local regulations and guidelines, and be mindful of your actions in the outdoors.


## 14.3 Wildlife Conservation

Switzerland is home to diverse wildlife, and conservation efforts play a vital role in protecting and keeping its natural habitats. Visitors can contribute to wildlife conservation by being responsible and respectful when meeting wildlife. Here are some key things to keep in mind for wildlife conservation in Switzerland:

**Observe Wildlife from a Distance**:
When encountering wildlife, keep a safe and respectful distance to avoid causing stress or disturbing their natural behavior. Use binoculars or a camera with a zoom lens for a better view.

**Do Not Feed Wildlife**:
Feeding wildlife can disrupt their natural foraging habits and lead to dependence on humans. Avoid feeding animals, as it can have negative effects on their health and behavior.

**Respect Habitat and Nesting Areas**:
Stay on marked trails and respect protected areas, including nesting sites and breeding grounds. These places are crucial for wildlife to raise their young and should be left undisturbed.

**Keep Wildlife Habitat Clean**:
Practice "Leave No Trace" concepts by carrying out any litter or waste and disposing of it properly. Leaving trash or food waste behind can draw wildlife and disrupt their natural behavior.

**Do Not Approach or Touch Wildlife**:
It's important to remember that wild animals are just that—wild. Never try to approach or touch wildlife, as it can be dangerous for both you and the animal. Respect their space and watch them from a safe distance.

**Stay Informed and Educated**:

Learn about the local wildlife species, their behaviors, and any specific guidelines or laws in place to protect them. Stay updated on conservation efforts and educational programs that support wildlife conservation.

**Support Conservation Organizations**:

Consider helping local wildlife conservation organizations through donations or volunteer work. These organizations play a crucial part in protecting and preserving Switzerland's wildlife and their habitats.

**Responsible Photography**:

When taking photos of wildlife, prioritize their well-being over getting the right shot. Use zoom lenses to keep a safe distance and avoid using flash photography, as it can startle or disturb animals.

**Report Wildlife Sightings**:

If you come across rare or endangered wildlife or witness any illegal activities related to wildlife, report your observations to the proper authorities. This helps add to monitoring and conservation efforts.

**Follow Local Regulations and Guidelines**:

Familiarize yourself with the local laws and guidelines regarding wildlife encounters, protected areas, and wildlife conservation. Respect these rules to ensure the well-being of the wildlife and their environments.

By following these rules, visitors can contribute to wildlife conservation efforts in Switzerland and help ensure the long-term survival and well-being of the country's diverse wildlife species.

## 14.4 Green Accommodation Options

Switzerland offers a range of green accommodation choices that prioritize sustainability, eco-friendliness, and responsible practices. Choosing green accommodations helps minimize your environmental effect and supports establishments that are committed to sustainability. Here are some green accommodation choices to consider when planning your trip:

**Eco-Friendly Hotels**:
Look for hotels that have adopted sustainable practices such as energy-efficient lighting, water conservation measures, waste management, and eco-friendly cleaning products.
Consider accommodations that have received eco-certifications such as the Swiss "Eco-label," which indicates their commitment to environmental responsibility.

**Green Bed and Breakfasts**:
Many bed and breakfast establishments in Switzerland value sustainability by using renewable energy, locally sourced products, and adopting waste reduction practices. These places often provide a more intimate and locally immersive experience.

**Eco-Lodges and Nature Retreats**:
For a closer connection to nature, try eco-lodges or nature retreats located in scenic locations. These accommodations are meant to have minimal impact on

the environment and often offer activities that promote environmental education and appreciation of nature.

**Sustainable Hostels**:

Hostels that prioritize sustainability often adopt practices such as energy-efficient lighting, recycling programs, and eco-friendly amenities. They provide budget-friendly choices for environmentally conscious travelers.

**Farm Stays**:

Experience sustainable living by choosing for farm stays, where you can immerse yourself in rural life and learn about organic farming practices. These accommodations often serve farm-to-table meals and offer chances for educational activities related to sustainable agriculture.

**Swiss Alpine Huts**:

For hikers and mountaineers, Swiss Alpine Huts offer rustic accommodations in beautiful mountain settings. Many huts follow sustainable practices, including solar energy use, waste reduction, and the use of local goods.

**Glamping**:

Enjoy a luxury camping experience with minimal environmental impact through glamping accommodations. These sites provide unique and comfortable accommodations in natural settings while incorporating eco-friendly practices.

**Certified Sustainable Accommodations**:

Look for accommodations that have achieved recognized sustainability certifications, such as the Swiss

"Minergie" certification for energy-efficient buildings or the "Zero Waste" certification for waste reduction efforts.

When booking accommodation, consider reaching out to the establishments directly to ask about their sustainability practices. Ask about their energy efficiency measures, waste management systems, use of renewable resources, and any other eco-friendly initiatives they have adopted.

By choosing green accommodation choices, you can minimize your environmental impact while enjoying a comfortable and memorable stay in Switzerland. Your conscious choices add to the overall sustainability of the tourism industry and support establishments that prioritize environmental responsibility.

# Traveling with Children

## 15.1 Family-friendly Activities and Attractions

Switzerland is an excellent destination for family travel, having a wide range of family-friendly activities and attractions that cater to children of all ages. Here are some of the top family-friendly activities you can enjoy in Switzerland:

**Adventure Parks and Theme Parks:**
Visit adventure parks such as Swiss Vapeur Parc, where kids can ride tiny steam trains, or Conny-Land, a fun-filled amusement park with rides, shows, and animal exhibits.

Explore theme parks like Chaplin's World, an interactive museum dedicated to Charlie Chaplin's life and work, or Technorama in Winterthur, a science and technology museum with hands-on exhibits.

**Animal Encounters**:
Take your children to wildlife parks and zoos like Zurich Zoo, Tierpark Goldau, or Basel Zoo, where they can watch a variety of animals up close and learn about conservation efforts.

Consider visiting Swiss Animal Parks, such as Arosa Bear Sanctuary or St. Bernard Dog Museum, to experience Swiss wildlife and learn about local animal customs.

**Boat Cruises**:
Enjoy family-friendly boat rides on Switzerland's beautiful lakes, such as Lake Geneva, Lake Lucerne, or Lake Zurich. Kids will love the beautiful views and the experience of being on a boat.

**Alpine Excursions**:
Take your family on cable car rides or funiculars to enjoy sweeping views of the Swiss Alps. Popular destinations include Mount Pilatus, Schilthorn, or Gornergrat, where you can view stunning mountain landscapes.

**Outdoor Adventures**:
Engage in outdoor activities good for families, such as hiking easy trails in places like the Lauterbrunnen Valley or Rigi Mountain. You can also go biking, horseback riding, or have a picnic in beautiful nature settings.

**Museums and Interactive Exhibits**:
Explore family-friendly museums like the Swiss Museum of Transport in Lucerne, where children can learn about different forms of transportation through interactive exhibits.

Visit the Museum of Natural History in Geneva or the Swiss Museum of Games in La Tour-de-Peilz for educational and interactive adventures.

**Swiss Chocolate and Cheese Experiences**:
Delight your children with visits to chocolate factories and cheese-making demonstrations, where they can learn about the Swiss culinary traditions and even join in

hands-on activities.

**Family-Friendly Cities**:

Explore towns like Zurich, Bern, or Lucerne, which offer a range of family-friendly attractions, including parks, playgrounds, and child-oriented museums.

**Festivals and Events**:

Check the local event calendar for family-friendly festivals and events going during your visit. The Fête de l'Escalade in Geneva and the Zibelemärit Onion Market in Bern are just a few examples.

Remember to check the age recommendations and any safety rules for each activity or attraction before planning your family adventures. Switzerland is known for its family-friendly setting and is sure to provide unforgettable experiences for both children and adults alike.

## 15.2 Theme Parks and Adventure

Switzerland offers a variety of theme parks and adventure sites that are perfect for families seeking thrilling experiences and fun-filled adventures. Here are some famous theme parks and adventure destinations to consider during your visit:

**Swiss Vapeur Parc (Le Bouveret):**

Enjoy a ride on tiny steam trains in a beautifully landscaped park. Swiss Vapeur Parc offers a unique experience for children and adults alike as you visit the park on these charming trains.

**Conny-Land (Lipperswil)**:

This amusement park is packed with rides, shows, and animal attractions. From roller coasters and water slides to a petting zoo and dolphin shows, Conny-Land offers fun for the whole family.

**Chaplin's World (Corsier-sur-Vevey)**:

Dive into the world of Charlie Chaplin at this interactive museum. Discover his life and work through multimedia displays, film shows, and re-creations of movie sets. Kids will love the full experience.

**Technorama (Winterthur):**

Technorama is a hands-on science and technology museum that sparks interest and learning. With over 500 interactive exhibits, children can explore various scientific phenomena and participate in educational experiments.

**Aquaparc (Le Bouveret):**

Cool off and have a blast at Aquaparc, a big indoor and outdoor water park. Enjoy exciting water slides, wave pools, and relaxation areas for a full day of aquatic fun.

Rope Parks and Adventure Courses:

Switzerland boasts numerous rope parks and adventure courses, such as Seilpark Interlaken, Forest Jump Switzerland, and Adventure Park Färich. These parks offer treetop adventures, zip lines, and challenging obstacle courses perfect for different age groups.

**Aventure Parc (Sion):**

Aventure Parc offers a range of outdoor sports, including tree climbing, zip-lining, and rope courses. It's an ideal destination for families wanting outdoor adventure and adrenaline-fueled fun.

**Glacier Adventure (Mount Titlis):**

Combine adventure with breathtaking alpine views at Mount Titlis. Take a revolving cable car to the top, walk through the Glacier Cave, and experience the thrilling Ice Flyer chairlift and Titlis Cliff Walk, Europe's highest suspension bridge.

**Swiss Mega Park (Bulle):**

Swiss Mega Park is a large indoor play area where children can jump on trampolines, handle obstacle courses, slide down giant slides, and enjoy an array of exciting games and activities.

These theme parks and adventure sites provide a mix of entertainment, educational experiences, and adrenaline-pumping thrills for families visiting Switzerland. Each park offers unique attractions, ensuring that children of all ages will have a memorable and enjoyable time during their stay.

## 15.3 Playgrounds

Switzerland offers numerous playgrounds throughout the country, providing children with chances for outdoor play and recreation. These playgrounds are well-maintained, safe, and made to cater to different age groups. Here are some famous playgrounds in Switzerland:

**Zurich**:

Irchelpark Playground: Located in Zurich, Irchelpark Playground offers a large wooden play structure, swings, sandboxes, and climbing equipment.

Mythenquai Playground: Situated along Lake Zurich, this playground offers a beautiful lakeside setting with slides, swings, and water play areas.

**Geneva**:

Parc La Grange Playground: Found in Parc La Grange, this playground features different play structures, sandboxes, and plenty of open space for children to run around.

Parc des Bastions Playground: Located near the Old Town, this playground offers a castle-themed play structure, swings, and climbing walls.

**Lucerne**:

Spielplatz Allmend: This big playground in Lucerne's Allmend area includes slides, swings, climbing structures, and even a small water play area.

Spielplatz Lido: Situated near Lake Lucerne, this playground includes a pirate ship-themed play structure, sandboxes, and a zip line.

**Bern**:

Rosengarten Playground: Found in the beautiful Rosengarten Park, this playground offers a range of play equipment, including swings, slides, and climbing frames.

Elfenau Playground: Located near the Elfenau Estate, this playground offers nature-inspired play structures, sand play areas, and plenty of green space.

**Basel**:

Kannenfeldpark Playground: Situated in Kannenfeldpark, this playground includes a big play structure, sandboxes, swings, and a water play area during the summer.

Solitude Park Playground: Found in Solitude Park, this playground offers a range of play equipment, including slides, climbing frames, and balancing elements.

These are just a few examples of the many parks available in Switzerland. You can also find playgrounds in smaller towns and rural areas, often found in parks or near residential areas. Playground facilities are usually well-equipped, safe, and provide a fun environment for children to play, socialize, and enjoy the outdoors during your visit to Switzerland.

## 15.4 Swiss Toy Museums

Switzerland is home to several toy museums that highlight the history, craftsmanship, and nostalgia of toys. These museums provide a delightful experience for both children and adults, giving a glimpse into the world of play and the evolution of toys. Here are some famous Swiss toy museums to explore:

**Swiss Museum of Games (La Tour-de-Peilz)**:
Located near Lake Geneva, the Swiss Museum of Games shows an extensive collection of traditional and modern games from around the world. Visitors can learn about the history, cultural importance, and evolution of games through interactive exhibits and displays.

Toy Museum (Basel):
The Toy Museum in Basel houses a remarkable collection of antique toys and shows the evolution of playthings over time. From dolls and teddy bears to model trains and cars, the museum gives a nostalgic journey into the world of toys.

**Teddy Bear Museum (Bern)**:
The Teddy Bear Museum in Bern is dedicated to these beloved cuddly pets. It shows a vast collection of teddy bears from different eras, showcasing their evolution and cultural significance. Visitors can enjoy exhibits, workshops, and even make their own teddy bears.

**Toy Worlds Museum (Sion)**:
The Toy Worlds Museum in Sion offers an immersive experience with its diverse collection of toys and models. Visitors can explore intricately designed dollhouses, miniature dioramas, and impressive toy collections from different eras.

**Spielzeug Welten Museum (Zurich)**:
Located in Zurich, the Spielzeug Welten Museum displays a wide range of toys, including dolls, model trains, tin toys, and more. The museum's collection

highlights the history of toy manufacturing and offers a nostalgic trip through the world of play.

**Ballenberg Open-Air Museum (Brienz):**

The Ballenberg Open-Air Museum in Brienz features a dedicated section called "House of Toys," where tourists can discover traditional Swiss toys and learn about local craftsmanship. The museum offers an interactive experience, allowing guests to try their hand at making wooden toys.

These toy museums provide a wonderful opportunity to explore the world of toys, admire their craftsmanship, and learn about their cultural and historical significance. Whether you're a toy enthusiast or simply looking for a fun and educational experience for the whole family, these museums offer a unique and delightful trip into the world of play.

## 15.5 Child-friendly Hiking and Outdoor Adventures

Switzerland is a paradise for outdoor lovers, and there are plenty of child-friendly hiking trails and outdoor adventures that the whole family can enjoy. These activities help children to connect with nature, learn about the environment, and create lasting memories. Here are some child-friendly hikes and outdoor adventures to consider during your visit:

**Männlichen-Kleine Scheidegg Panorama Trail**

**(Grindelwald):**

This easy and scenic walk offers breathtaking views of the Eiger, Mönch, and Jungfrau mountains. It's suitable for families with children, as the trail is well-maintained and offers different resting points along the way.

**Oeschinensee Lake (Kandersteg):**

Take a leisurely walk to the picturesque Oeschinensee Lake, surrounded by towering mountains. The trail is manageable for children and offers the chance to enjoy a picnic by the lake or rent rowboats for a fun family adventure.

Trümmelbach Falls (Lauterbrunnen):

Visit the Trümmelbach Falls, a series of impressive waterfalls inside the mountain. Children will be fascinated by the thundering cascades and the unique experience of walking through the mountain to watch the power of nature.

**Aare Gorge (Meiringen):**

Explore the Aare Gorge, a natural wonder made by the Aare River. The well-maintained trail takes you through narrow passages and over bridges, giving a thrilling and educational experience for children.

**Rhine Falls (Schaffhausen):**

Visit the magnificent Rhine Falls, the biggest waterfall in Europe. Children can marvel at the powerful cascades, take a boat ride to the rock in the middle of the falls, and enjoy the adventure park located nearby.

**Muggestutz Trail (Lenk):**

The Muggestutz Trail is a themed hiking trail that follows the tales of the Swiss gnome, Muggestutz. Children can follow the story and enjoy various interactive places along the way, making the hike entertaining and engaging.

**Swiss National Park (Zernez)**:

Explore the Swiss National Park, a protected area filled with wildlife and natural beauty. Children can start on guided tours and educational programs to learn about the park's ecosystems and the importance of conservation.

**Forest Adventure Park (Zurich)**:

Visit the Forest Adventure Park in Zurich, where children can enjoy zip lines, rope courses, and other outdoor challenges perfect for their age. The park offers a safe and exciting environment for kids to try their agility and have fun in nature.

Before going on any outdoor activity, ensure that the trail or adventure is suitable for your children's age and abilities. It's important to dress appropriately, carry water and snacks, and prioritize safety during your outdoor adventures. Switzerland's pristine landscapes provide a great backdrop for family exploration and outdoor bonding experiences.

# Traveling with Disabilities

## 16.1 Accessibility in Switzerland

Switzerland is dedicated to providing accessibility and ensuring that travelers with disabilities can enjoy their visit to the fullest. Efforts have been made to improve accessibility in various areas, including transportation, accommodation, and tourist sites. Here is a breakdown of accessibility in Switzerland:

**Transportation**:

Public Transportation: Swiss public transportation, including trains, trams, and buses, usually offers good accessibility for people with disabilities. Many stations and vehicles are equipped with ramps or lifts, and designated places are available for wheelchair users.

Taxis: Accessible taxis with ramps or lifts are available in big cities and can be pre-booked for transportation. It's advisable to call local taxi companies in advance to ensure availability.

Car Rentals: Several car rental companies in Switzerland offer vehicles with adaptations for people with disabilities, such as hand controls or wheelchair mobility. It's recommended to inquire and book in advance to reserve a suitable vehicle.

Accessible Facilities: Some hotels offer extra facilities such as accessible entrances, elevators, and common areas. However, it's important to check with the hotel in advance to ensure that their accessibility meets your unique needs.

**Tourist Attractions**:

Museums and Cultural Sites: Several museums and cultural sites in Switzerland have made efforts to improve accessibility, including providing ramps, lifts, and accessible restrooms. However, it's recommended to check the specific accessibility features of each attraction before going.

Natural Parks and Scenic Areas: While some natural parks and mountain areas may present challenges due to rugged terrain, efforts have been made to improve accessibility in certain places. For example, some mountain cable cars and funiculars offer wheelchair access, allowing tourists with disabilities to enjoy the stunning alpine landscapes.

**Support and Resources**:

Swiss Travel Pass: The Swiss Travel Pass gives unlimited travel on the Swiss Travel System network and provides discounts on different attractions. It's worth considering this pass, as it can simplify travel arrangements and provide cost savings for people with disabilities.

Accessibility Information: Tourist offices and official websites provide information on accessibility features and services available at different destinations. Additionally, it's recommended to call specific attractions or accommodation providers directly to ask about their accessibility features.

While Switzerland strives to provide accessibility, it's important to plan your trip in advance and communicate any specific needs or requirements to ensure a smooth and enjoyable experience. By doing so, travelers with disabilities can discover Switzerland's beauty, cultural heritage, and outdoor adventures with greater ease and comfort.

## 16.2Wheelchair-friendly Attractions and Facilities

Switzerland offers a range of wheelchair-friendly attractions and facilities to ensure that people with mobility challenges can fully enjoy their visit. Here are some wheelchair-friendly sites and facilities in Switzerland:

**Museums and Cultural Sites**:
Swiss Museum of Transport (Lucerne): This museum offers wheelchair-accessible entrances, elevators, and spacious halls. Some exhibits provide tactile features for visitors with visual impairments.

Museum of Art (Zurich): The museum is provided with ramps and elevators for wheelchair access, and accessible restrooms are available.

Olympic Museum (Lausanne): This museum offers wheelchair-accessible entrances, elevators, and accessible restrooms. Wheelchair users can explore the exhibits and enjoy interactive displays.

**Scenic Attractions**:

Mount Titlis (Engelberg): The rotating cable car to Mount Titlis is wheelchair accessible, and there are ramps and stairs at the summit station. The viewing platforms and restaurants are accessible, giving amazing panoramic views.

Rhine Falls (Schaffhausen): Wheelchair users can reach different viewpoints of the falls, and there are designated parking spaces and accessible pathways. Some boat tours also provide wheelchair-accessible choices.

**City Tours**:

Zurich: The Zurich Tourism Office offers a brochure on wheelchair-accessible tours, highlighting accessible routes, attractions, and transportation choices.

Geneva: The Geneva Tourism Office offers information on wheelchair-accessible tours, including accessible routes and sites in the city.

**National Parks and Scenic Areas**:

Swiss National Park (Zernez): The visitor center, some trails, and viewing spots in the park are wheelchair accessible. The park also offers guided tours suitable for wheelchair users.

Schynige Platte (Interlaken): The cogwheel train to Schynige Platte is wheelchair accessible, and the mountain-top botanical garden is accessible via paved paths.

**Public Transportation**:

Swiss Federal Railways (SBB): Most SBB trains give designated wheelchair spaces, accessible restrooms, and ramps or lifts for easy boarding. Stations are equipped with stairs or ramps for accessibility.

Local Public Transportation: Many local buses and trams in Swiss towns have low floors for easy wheelchair access. Stations and stops often have ramps or lifts, and visual and audio announcements are given.

**Accessibility in Cities**:

Zurich, Geneva, and Basel: These cities have made efforts to improve accessibility by offering wheelchair-accessible public transportation, ramps, and elevators in public buildings, and accessible pedestrian areas.

It's important to note that while Switzerland strives to provide wheelchair accessibility, the amount of accessibility may vary between attractions and locations. It's suggested to contact specific attractions or consult their official websites for detailed accessibility information and to ensure a smooth and enjoyable experience.

Additionally, it's advisable to tell transportation providers and accommodation establishments of your specific needs in advance, as they may be able to provide extra assistance or make necessary arrangements to accommodate wheelchair users.

By planning ahead and utilizing the available wheelchair-friendly sites and facilities, individuals with mobility challenges can explore Switzerland's diverse landscapes, cultural treasures, and city delights with greater accessibility and convenience.

## 16.3 Special Assistance Services

Switzerland provides special assistance services to ensure that travelers with disabilities have a comfortable and enjoyable experience during their stay. These services aim to support individuals with specific needs and help them navigate through different aspects of their trip. Here are some special assistance services offered in Switzerland:

**Airport Assistance**:

Swiss airports, including Zurich Airport and Geneva Airport, offer special assistance services for passengers with disabilities. These services may include wheelchair assistance, priority boarding, and dedicated assistance staff to guide passengers through security checks and boarding processes. It's recommended to call your airline or the respective airport in advance to arrange for assistance.

**Wheelchair Rental**:

In major cities and tourist locations, it's possible to rent wheelchairs or mobility aids from specialized providers. This allows visitors with mobility challenges to explore attractions and navigate through the city with ease. It's recommended to book in advance to ensure availability.

**Guided Tours**:

Several tour operators and tourist offices in Switzerland offer guided tours specifically created for individuals with disabilities. These tours take into consideration accessibility standards and provide expert guides who can cater to the needs of participants. It's recommended to inquire with local tour operators or tourist offices about available choices.

**Accessible Accommodation**:

Many hotels in Switzerland provide accessible rooms equipped with features such as widened doorways, grab bars, and accessible baths. When booking accommodation, it's advisable to tell the hotel about your specific needs to ensure that they can accommodate your requirements.

**Accessibility Information**:

Tourist offices and official websites provide information on accessibility features and services offered at different destinations. This includes details on accessible attractions, public transportation, and facilities. It's recommended to consult these tools and plan your itinerary properly.

**Accessible Transportation**:

Swiss public transportation, including trains, trams, and buses, usually offer accessibility features, such as ramps, lifts, and designated wheelchair spaces. Some towns also provide accessible taxis with ramps or lifts. It's advisable to familiarize yourself with the accessibility features of public transportation and call local transportation providers for any specific assistance needed.

**Personal Assistance**:

If you require personal assistance during your trip, such as a caregiver or companion, it's recommended to plan for these services in advance. Some travel agencies or specialized service providers can help in coordinating personal assistance based on your specific requirements.

When planning your trip, it's important to communicate your unique needs and requirements to relevant service providers, including airlines, accommodation establishments, and tour operators. Providing them with detailed information will help them to offer appropriate assistance and make necessary arrangements to ensure a smooth and enjoyable travel experience.

Switzerland tries to make travel accessible for all, and with the assistance services available, individuals with disabilities can explore the country's beauty, cultural heritage, and outdoor adventures with greater comfort and support.

# Tips for Solo Travelers

## 17.1 Safety and Security Tips

Traveling solo can be an exciting and powerful experience. To ensure your safety and security while visiting Switzerland, consider the following tips:

**Research your destination**: Before your trip, research the location you plan to visit. Familiarize yourself with local customs, traditions, and any safety worries or travel advisories. Understanding the local culture and being aware of potential risks can help you make informed choices.

**Share your itinerary**: Inform a trusted friend or family member about your trip plans, including your itinerary, accommodation details, and contact information. Regularly update them on your whereabouts, especially if you change your plans. This way, someone back home knows where you are in case of an accident.

**Stay connected**: Carry a fully charged mobile phone and keep important contacts saved, including emergency contacts and the contact information of your office or consulate. Ensure you have a reliable means of contact throughout your trip.

**Be cautious with personal information**: Avoid sharing too much personal information with strangers, especially in public places. Exercise caution when using social media and avoid sharing real-time updates that could compromise your safety or suggest that you are traveling alone.

**Trust your feelings**: Your instincts are a valuable guide. If something feels off or unsafe, remove yourself from the setting. Trust your gut feelings and value your well-being.

**Stay in well-reviewed accommodations**: Choose accommodations with positive reviews and good security measures. Check if they have 24-hour reception, secure entry, and well-lit common areas. Inform the front desk about your solo journey and any specific concerns you may have.

**Use reliable transportation:** Opt for licensed taxis or reputable ride-sharing services when going within cities. Avoid accepting rides from unmarked vehicles or people who approach you on the street. When using public transportation, be aware of your surroundings and keep an eye on your things.

**Stay vigilant with your belongings**: Keep your valuables, such as passports, money, and electronics, safe at all times. Consider using a money belt or a secure bag to keep your important papers and belongings close to you. Be mindful of pickpockets in crowded areas and avoid displaying expensive things openly.

**Blend in with the locals**: Try to blend in with the local culture by dressing modestly and respecting local customs and practices. Being mindful of cultural norms can help you avoid unnecessary attention and possible misunderstandings.

**Stay informed about local laws and regulations**: Familiarize yourself with the local laws and regulations of the places you plan to visit. Adhere to them and respect local customs and traditions to avoid any legal problems.

**Use reputable tour operators and guides**: If you plan to join in guided tours or adventure activities, choose reputable tour operators with good reviews and safety records. Ensure that they value the safety and well-being of their participants.

**Stay in public and well-lit areas**: Especially at night, stick to well-populated and well-lit areas. Avoid walking alone in secluded or poorly lit areas, and be cautious when taking invitations or offers from strangers.

Remember, solo travel can be incredibly rewarding, but it's important to prioritize your safety and well-being. By taking precautions, staying aware of your surroundings, and following your instincts, you can enjoy a memorable and safe solo adventure in Switzerland.

## 17.2 Joining Group Tours and Activities

Joining group tours and activities as a solo traveler can enhance your travel experience and provide chances for social interaction. Here are some tips for joining group trips and activities:

**Research tour options**: Look for group tours and

activities that fit with your interests and preferences. Consider the size of the group, the length of the tour, and the specific activities included. Read reviews and gather information to ensure that the tour or activity is reputable and good for solo travelers.

**Choose solo-friendly tours**: Some tour operators specialize in catering to solo travelers or offer group tours that are welcoming to people traveling alone. Look for tours that clearly note their suitability for solo travelers or inquire with the tour operator about their policies regarding solo participants.

**Meet fellow travelers**: Group tours provide an excellent chance to meet other like-minded travelers. Be open to connecting with fellow tour participants, strike up conversations, and create new friendships. Remember that everyone is in the same boat, eager to explore and experience the location.

**Stay engaged**: Participate actively in the tour or exercise. Ask questions, add to discussions, and immerse yourself in the experience. Engaging with the group and the tour guide improves the overall experience and makes it more enjoyable.

**Be respectful and considerate**: Remember to respect the tour guide, fellow participants, and the local customs. Be mindful of others' preferences, personal space, and views. Respect any rules or guidelines set by the tour operator and follow their directions throughout the tour.

**Exchange contact information**: If you connect with

other solo travelers during the tour, consider sharing contact information. This way, you can stay in touch, share travel tips, and even plan future trips together.

**Be flexible and open-minded**: Group tours bring together people from various backgrounds and with different travel ways. Embrace the diversity and be open to new situations and perspectives. Being flexible and adaptable can make the group tour experience more fun.

**Plan some solo time**: While group trips are great for socializing, it's also important to have some solo time during your travels. Use the free time outside of the tour plan to explore independently, visit attractions that interest you personally, or simply relax and recharge.

Provide feedback: After the tour or activity, consider giving feedback to the tour operator. Share your experience, highlight any positive aspects, and give constructive feedback if appropriate. This helps the tour operator improve their services and ensures that future solo tourists have a great experience.

Group tours and activities can enrich your solo travel experience by offering chances for social interaction, shared experiences, and a sense of community. By selecting tours that cater to solo travelers, staying involved, and being open to meeting new people, you can make lasting connections and create unforgettable memories during your time in Switzerland.

## 17.3 Meeting Fellow Travelers

As a solo traveler, meeting fellow travelers can add a social dimension to your trip and create chances for shared experiences and new friendships. Here are some tips for meeting fellow travelers:

**Stay in social accommodations**: Choose accommodations that have common areas such as lounges, communal kitchens, or social places where travelers can connect. Hostels, guesthouses, and some budget hotels often provide these services, making it easier to meet and connect with other travelers.

**Participate in group activities**: Join group activities or organized tours that encourage interaction among members. This could include city walking tours, adventure trips, cooking classes, or group hikes. These events provide a platform to meet fellow travelers who share similar interests.

**Use social networking apps**: Utilize social networking apps made for travelers, such as Travello, Backpackr, or Meetup. These platforms allow you to connect with fellow tourists, find local events, or join group meetups. You can attend social gatherings or explore the destination together with like-minded people.

**Join online travel communities**: Engage in online travel communities and forums, such as travel-related Facebook groups, travel boards, or travel-specific websites. These platforms provide chances to connect with fellow travelers, seek advice, and possibly meet up with others who are traveling to the same destination.

**Attend local events and gatherings**: Keep an eye out for local events, fairs, or gatherings happening during your visit. These events often attract both locals and travelers, making an ideal setting to mingle and meet new people.

**Visit communal spaces**: Hang out in communal spaces such as parks, cafes, or public places. These areas often draw both locals and travelers, giving a casual setting for conversations and interactions.

**Engage in group activities or classes**: Enroll in group activities or classes that interest you, such as language lessons, cooking workshops, or yoga sessions. These activities provide a chance to meet individuals with similar hobbies or passions.

**Strike up conversations**: Be open and friendly. Initiate conversations with fellow travelers you meet during your trip, whether it's in accommodation common areas, on public transportation, or at popular attractions. A simple "hello" or asking for suggestions can lead to interesting conversations and connections.

**Attend social nights or hostel events**: Many hostels organize social nights or events where travelers can gather, socialize, and share travel stories. Take advantage of these chances to meet fellow travelers in a relaxed and friendly atmosphere.

**Be open to invitations**: If you receive invitations from fellow travelers or locals to join them for an activity, meal, or outing, be open to talking. It can lead to memorable adventures and the chance to forge new friendships.

Remember to use your judgment and value your safety when meeting fellow travelers. Trust your instincts and take necessary measures when interacting with strangers. By being open, friendly, and proactive in seeking opportunities to meet fellow travelers, you can enhance your solo travel experience and make meaningful connections along the way.

# Language and Culture Guides

## 18.1 Basic German Phrases

Germany is one of the official languages spoken in Switzerland, and knowing some basic German phrases can greatly improve your travel experience. Here are some important phrases to help you communicate with locals:

**Greetings and Basic Expressions**:
Hello: Hallo
Good morning: Guten Morgen
Good afternoon: Guten Tag
Good evening: Guten Abend
Goodbye: Auf Wiedersehen
Thank you: Danke
Yes: Ja
No: Nein
Please: Bitte
Excuse me: Entschuldigung
I'm sorry: Es tut mir leid
Introductions and Polite Phrases:
My name is...: Mein Name ist...
What is your name?: Wie heißen Sie?
Nice to meet you: Es freut mich, Sie kennenzulernen
How are you?: Wie geht es Ihnen?
I don't understand: Ich verstehe nicht
Could you please speak slower?: Könnten Sie bitte langsamer sprechen?
Directions and Transportation:
Where is...?: Wo ist...?
How do I get to...?: Wie komme ich nach...?
Train station: Bahnhof
Bus stop: Bushaltestelle

Left: Links

Right: Rechts

Straight ahead: Geradeaus

Excuse me, is this place taken?: Entschuldigen Sie, ist dieser Platz frei?

Dining and Food:

I would like...: Ich hätte gerne...

The menu, please: Die Speisekarte, bitte

I'm a vegetarian: Ich bin Vegetarier/Vegetarierin

Do you have any recommendations?: Haben Sie Empfehlungen?

May I have the bill, please?: Kann ich bitte die Rechnung haben?

Shopping and Shopping Phrases:

How much does it cost?: Wie viel kostet das?

Can I put it on?: Kann ich es anprobieren?

Do you take credit cards?: Akzeptieren Sie Kreditkarten?

I'm just browsing: Ich schaue mich nur um

Emergency Phrases:

Help!: Hilfe!

I need a doctor: Ich brauche einen Arzt/eine Ärztin

Where is the best hospital?: Wo ist das nächste Krankenhaus?

Call the police: Rufen Sie die Polizei an

Remember, making an effort to speak even a few simple phrases in German shows respect and can help you connect with locals. Don't be afraid to try, and most importantly, have fun visiting Switzerland while immersing yourself in its rich language and culture!

## 18.2 Basic French Phrases

French is another official language spoken in Switzerland, especially in the western region. Knowing some simple French phrases can be helpful during your travels. Here are some important phrases to assist you in communicating with locals:

**Greetings and Basic Expressions**:

Hello: Bonjour

Good morning: Bonjour (used throughout the day)

Good evening: Bonsoir

Goodbye: Au revoir

Thank you: Merci

Yes: Oui

No: Non

Please: S'il vous plaît

Excuse me: Excusez-moi

I'm sorry: Je suis désolé(e)

Introductions and Polite Phrases:

My name is...: Je m'appelle...

What is your name?: Comment vous appelez-vous?

Nice to meet you: Enchanté(e)

How are you?: Comment ça va?

I don't understand: Je ne comprends pas

Could you please speak slower?: Pouvez-vous parler plus lentement, s'il vous plaît?

Directions and Transportation:

Where is...?: Où est...?

How do I get to...?: Comment puis-je me rendre à...?

Train station: Gare (SNCF)

Bus stop: Arrêt de bus

Left: À gauche

Right: À droite

Straight ahead: Tout droit

Excuse me, is this place taken?: Excusez-moi, cette place est-elle prise?

Dining and Food:

I would like...: Je voudrais...

The menu, please: La carte, s'il vous plaît

I'm a vegetarian: Je suis végétarien(ne)

Do you have any recommendations?: Avez-vous des recommandations?

May I have the bill, please?: L'addition, s'il vous plaît

Shopping and Shopping Phrases:

How much does it cost?: Combien ça coûte?

Can I put it on?: Est-ce que je peux l'essayer?

Do you take credit cards?: Acceptez-vous les cartes de crédit?

I'm just browsing: Je regarde simplement

**Emergency Phrases**:

Help!: À l'aide!

I need a doctor: J'ai besoin d'un médecin

Where is the best hospital?: Où se trouve l'hôpital le plus proche?

Call the police: Appelez la police
Using these basic French phrases will show your efforts to communicate and connect with locals, making your travel experience in Switzerland more enjoyable. Embrace the chance to practice your French skills and immerse yourself in the local culture!

## 18.3 Basic Italian Phrases

Italian is one of the official languages spoken in Switzerland, especially in the southern region. Knowing some simple Italian phrases can enhance your travel experience and help you interact with locals. Here are some important phrases to assist you:

**Greetings and Basic Expressions**:
Hello: Ciao
Good morning: Buongiorno
Good evening: Buonasera
Goodbye: Arrivederci
Thank you: Grazie
Yes: Sì
No: No
Please: Per favore
Excuse me: Mi scusi
I'm sorry: Mi dispiace
Introductions and Polite Phrases:
My name is...: Mi chiamo...
What is your name?: Come si chiama?

Nice to meet you: Piacere di conoscerla

How are you?: Come sta?

I don't understand: Non capisco

Could you please speak slower?: Potrebbe parlare più lentamente, per favore?

Directions and Transportation:

Where is...?: Dove si trova...?

How do I get to...?: Come arrivo a...?

Train station: Stazione ferroviaria

Bus stop: Fermata dell'autobus

Left: A sinistra

Right: A destra

Straight ahead: Sempre dritto

Excuse me, is this place taken?: Mi scusi, è occupato questo posto?

Dining and Food:

I would like...: Vorrei...

The menu, please: Il menù, per favore

I'm a vegetarian: Sono vegetariano/vegetariana

Do you have any recommendations?: Ha delle raccomandazioni?

May I have the bill, please?: Mi può portare il conto, per favore?

**Shopping and Shopping Phrases**:

How much does it cost?: Quanto costa?

Can I put it on?: Posso provarlo?

Do you take credit cards?: Accettate le carte di credito?

I'm just browsing: Sto solo guardando

**Emergency Phrases**:

Help!: Aiuto!

I need a doctor: Ho bisogno di un dottore

Where is the best hospital?: Dove si trova l'ospedale più vicino?

Call the police: Chiami la polizia

Using these basic Italian phrases will allow you to navigate through Italy's linguistic landscape, even in the Swiss areas where Italian is spoken. It shows your effort to connect with locals and engage yourself in the local culture. Enjoy your travels in Switzerland and embrace the chance to practice your Italian!

## 18.4 Swiss-German Dialects

Swiss-German dialects are a group of Alemannic dialects spoken in different regions of Switzerland. While Standard German is the official language, Swiss-German dialects are widely used in everyday conversation among the local population. Here are some **key points about Swiss-German dialects**:

Variations and Regional Differences: Swiss-German dialects vary greatly across different regions of Switzerland. Each canton, and even smaller places within cantons, may have its own distinct dialect with unique vocabulary, pronunciation, and grammar. Some well-known languages include Zürich German, Basel German, and Bernese German.

Pronunciation: Swiss-German dialects often feature different pronunciation patterns compared to Standard German. The sounds and intonation can differ greatly, making it challenging for non-native speakers to understand and reproduce. Additionally, vowel sounds and consonant shifts can vary across different languages.

Vocabulary: Swiss-German dialects have their own vocabulary that varies from Standard German. Many words and phrases are specific to the area and may not be widely understood in other parts of Switzerland or Germany. This includes everyday terms, slang, and local phrases that add color and uniqueness to the dialects.

Written Form: Swiss-German dialects are mainly spoken languages, and there is no standardized written form for these dialects. Swiss-German is usually used in informal communication, such as personal conversations, text messages, and social media posts. In more formal or official settings, Standard German is used for written dialogue.

Familiarity and Understanding: Swiss-German dialects can be difficult for non-native speakers to understand, especially if they have learned Standard German. The vocabulary, pronunciation, and grammar differences may take some time to become accustomed to. However, Swiss people are usually familiar with Standard German and can switch to it when communicating with non-native speakers.

Cultural Significance: Swiss-German dialects play an

important role in Swiss society and identity. They are strongly rooted in local traditions, customs, and regional pride. Speaking and understanding the local dialect can help create a stronger connection with the local community and improve your cultural experience in Switzerland.

While it may be challenging to learn and fully grasp Swiss-German dialects, locals appreciate the effort when visitors try to use some of the dialect words or expressions. Don't hesitate to interact with locals and ask them about their dialect or specific vocabulary. It can be a fun way to immerse yourself in the local culture and make meaningful connections during your time in Switzerland.

# Useful Resources and Contacts

## 19.1 Tourist Information Centers

When visiting Switzerland, tourist information centers can be invaluable sources of local knowledge, maps, brochures, and help. Here are some good resources and contacts to help you find tourist information centers:

**Switzerland Tourism**:

Website: www.myswitzerland.com

Switzerland Tourism is the main tourism organization of Switzerland. Their website provides thorough information about destinations, attractions, activities, accommodations, and travel tips.

**Regional Tourist Offices**:

Each region in Switzerland usually has its own tourist office that provides detailed information about local attractions, events, transportation, and more. These offices are excellent resources for planning your itinerary and obtaining up-to-date information about particular regions.

**Local City Tourist Offices**:

Most major towns in Switzerland have their own tourist offices, located centrally and easily accessible. These offices provide detailed information about city sites, tours, public transportation, and other services.

Online Resources:

Various online platforms give extensive information about Switzerland, including travel blogs, forums, and review websites. These platforms can provide insights and suggestions from fellow travelers who have visited Switzerland.

**Mobile Applications**:

Downloading travel apps specific to Switzerland can be helpful for viewing offline maps, public transportation schedules, language translation, and other useful features. Some famous apps include SBB Mobile (for train schedules), Swiss Travel Guide, and Tripadvisor.

Emergency Contacts:

In case of emergencies, it's important to have the necessary contacts easily available. The emergency number in Switzerland is 112 for all emergencies, including police, fire, and medical help.

**Local Transport Contacts**:

Depending on the area, different transportation providers may operate within Switzerland, such as Swiss Federal Railways (SBB), regional bus companies, or mountain cable cars. Note down the appropriate contact information for these services to inquire about schedules, fares, and any disruptions.

It's always recommended to check the official websites or call the relevant tourist information centers directly to obtain the most accurate and up-to-date information. These tools will ensure that you have access to comprehensive information and expert assistance to make the most of your trip to Switzerland.

## 19.2 Embassies and Consulates

In case you require assistance from your home country's foreign missions while in Switzerland, it's important to have information about the relevant embassies and consulates. Here are some tools and contacts to help you find embassies and consulates in Switzerland:

Your Home Country's Embassy or Consulate in **Switzerland**:

Contact your country's embassy or consulate in Switzerland for help with passport problems, consular services, emergency support, and other related matters. They can provide guidance and support unique to your nationality.

**Embassy/Consulate Directories**:

Visit the website of the Federal Department of Foreign Affairs (FDFA) of Switzerland (www.eda.admin.ch) for a list of embassies and consulates in Switzerland. This directory gives contact details and addresses of foreign embassies and consulates based in Switzerland.

**Embassy/Consulate Websites**:

Visit the official websites of your home country's embassy or consulate in Switzerland for full information on their services, contact information, office hours, and emergency contact numbers. These websites often provide helpful information for citizens traveling or living abroad.

**Emergency Contacts**:

In case of emergency situations involving your home country's citizens, call the local embassy or consulate immediately. They can provide advice and assistance in emergencies such as accidents, lost passports, or other critical situations.

It is advisable to register with your home country's

embassy or consulate before your trip, especially if you plan to stay in Switzerland for an extended time. This helps them to have your contact details and provide relevant updates or assistance when necessary.

Remember to keep important documents such as your passport, identification, and emergency contact information secure yet easily available during your travels. In case of any emergency or need for assistance, reach out to the appropriate embassy or consulate immediately for guidance and support.

## 19.3 Online Travel Resources

When planning your trip to Switzerland, online travel resources can provide valuable information, suggestions, and tools to make your journey smoother. Here are some popular online travel resources to help you:

**Official Tourism Websites**:

Switzerland Tourism (www.myswitzerland.com): The official tourism website of Switzerland offers comprehensive information about destinations, attractions, activities, accommodations, and travel tips.

**Travel Booking Platforms**:

Expedia (www.expedia.com), Booking.com (www.booking.com), and Airbnb (www.airbnb.com): These platforms offer a wide range of choices for booking flights, accommodations, car rentals, and vacation rentals in Switzerland.

**Travel Forums and Communities**:
TripAdvisor (www.tripadvisor.com) and Lonely Planet Thorn Tree Forum (www.lonelyplanet.com/thorntree): These online travel communities allow you to seek help, read reviews, and interact with fellow travelers who have visited Switzerland.

**Travel Blogs and Websites**:
Nomadic Matt (www.nomadicmatt.com), The Blonde Abroad (www.theblondeabroad.com), and Adventurous Kate (www.adventurouskate.com): These famous travel blogs provide detailed guides, itineraries, and personal experiences in Switzerland.

**Travel Apps**:
Swiss Travel Guide (by Triposo) and Switzerland Mobility (for hiking and biking routes): These mobile apps offer detailed travel guides, offline maps, local recommendations, and useful information about Switzerland.

**Social Media Platforms**:
Instagram, Facebook, and YouTube: Follow travel influencers, tourism boards, and Switzerland-specific accounts to discover stunning pictures, travel tips, and inspiring content related to Switzerland.

**Online Language Tools**:
Duolingo (www.duolingo.com) and Babbel (www.babbel.com): These language-learning platforms can help you brush up on important phrases in German, French, or Italian, which are spoken in different regions

of Switzerland.

**Travel Insurance Providers**:

World Nomads (www.worldnomads.com), Allianz Global Assistance (www.allianztravelinsurance.com), and AXA (www.axa.com): These companies offer travel insurance coverage for medical problems, trip cancellations, and other unforeseen events during your stay in Switzerland.

When using online travel resources, it's important to cross-reference information and read various reviews to get a well-rounded perspective. Remember to consult government websites, local authorities, and reputable sources for the most up-to-date and accurate information regarding travel guidelines, safety measures, and entry requirements for Switzerland.

By utilizing these online travel resources, you can gather valuable insights, plan your itinerary, and make informed choices to ensure a memorable and enjoyable trip to Switzerland.

## 19.4 Emergency Contacts in Switzerland

It's important to prepare yourself with emergency contacts in Switzerland to ensure your safety and well-being during your trip. Here are some important emergency contacts:

**General Emergency Number**:

Dial 112 for all emergencies, including police, fire, and

medical help. This number is valid throughout Switzerland and connects you to the proper emergency services.

**Police**:

For non-emergency police help, dial 117.

Ambulance and Medical Emergencies:

Dial 144 for medical emergencies, including urgent medical help, ambulance services, and rescue operations.

**Fire Department**:

In case of a fire or fire-related emergency, dial 118 to contact the fire service.

**Mountain Rescue**:

If you are hiking, skiing, or participating in outdoor activities in the mountains and require rescue or assistance, dial 1414 for mountain rescue services.

**Poison Control**:

In case of poisoning or toxic exposures, call the Swiss Toxicological Information Center by dialing 145.

Roadside Assistance:

If you face car troubles or require roadside assistance, call the TCS (Touring Club Switzerland) helpline at 140.

**Helicopter Rescue**:

In remote areas or mountainous regions, helicopter rescue may be necessary for medical situations. Dial 1414 to request helicopter relief services.

It is recommended to save these emergency contact numbers in your phone or keep them easily accessible. Additionally, it's important to have travel insurance that covers medical situations, as well as knowing the details of your insurance coverage.

In case of any emergency situation, stay calm, provide clear information about your location and the nature of the emergency, and follow the instructions given by the emergency services.

Please note that while the provided emergency contact numbers are up-to-date at the time of this guide's release, it's always wise to check with local authorities or official sources for any updates or changes to emergency contact information in Switzerland.

# NOT PARAPHRASED